Praise for Michael

ROAR

"*ROAR* is a delight. The wisdom it offers working adults of all ages is compassionate, results-driven, and eminently actionable. Whether you're making a midlife career change or seeking purpose after retirement, you couldn't pick a better road map for your next chapter than *ROAR*. It will teach you how to approach the future not with fear or worry, but with passion and purpose."

—**Michael Sebastian**, editor in chief of *Esquire*

"Many of us achieve big goals in the first half of our lives and then we hit a certain age and struggle with the question: What's next for me? Well, guess what? Your best days are ahead of you, and this book will help you find clarity on your vision, purpose, and passion. *ROAR* provides the trail map to get you on track to live the rest of your life without limits."

—**Alison Levine**, team captain of the first American women's Everest expedition and *New York Times* bestselling author of *On the Edge*

"Joining the ranks of Brené Brown and Elizabeth Gilbert, Michael Clinton forces you to evaluate your life honestly and embrace radical solutions for what's not working. Brimming with real-life examples, he gives a blueprint for how to embrace your second act that will ensure you ROAR as loud as you can."

—**Joanna Coles**, executive producer *The Bold Type* and director of Snap, Inc.

"With *ROAR*, Michael Clinton provides a thoroughly engaging, galvanizing guide to getting past roadblocks and making the most of your next chapter. The book is packed with inspiring examples of people who reimagined their lives, although none more inspiring than Clinton himself, who rose from humble origins to become a revered executive, philanthropist, photographer, and so much more. A page-turner written with warmth and wit, *ROAR* will help you find your purpose while leaving little doubt that the best is yet to come."

—**Lucy Kaylin**, vice president of print content at Hearst Magazines

"As a forty-year-plus veteran of the 'mad men' world of advertising, I found *ROAR* to be compelling and inspirational on my own journey to reimagine and re-create my next chapter(s)."

—**Bob Jeffrey**, former chairman and CEO of J. Walter Thompson

"Are you yearning for the best second half of your life ever? Well, here's the secret sauce you've been waiting for. Michael Clinton's *ROAR* is chock-full of absolutely terrific real-life inspiration, wisdom, and strategies to finally make it happen— starting NOW."

—**Kate White**, former editor in chief of *Cosmopolitan* and *New York Times* bestselling suspense author

"Wondering what to do in the second half of your life? Wonder no more. Michael Clinton's latest book *ROAR* is an indispensable guide to what can be and should be your next chapter. *ROAR* is not for dreamers. It is for doers who are not content to watch the world pass them by. So don't just sit there...ROAR!"

—**Pamela Fiori**, author and former editor in chief of *Town & Country*

"This book is a gift for anyone navigating the challenges of personal reinvention. Its compelling format recounts the varied paths of so many successful people who have pivoted to new careers and passions. In that way it is also a guidebook that offers instructive planning tools. Most important, it reminds us that our greatest asset is knowing ourselves through careful self-evaluation. That is the catalyst for the journey of reinvention and enables us to do so with confidence and passion! Bonus—this subject matter is not the provenance for only those aged 50+. *ROAR*'s inspirational insights are valuable to people of every age who are brave enough to reimagine themselves and their lives in new ways."

—**Kevin C. O'Malley**, former media executive and current entertainment industry entrepreneur

"I am not exaggerating when I say this book will change your life. Drawing on Michael's own story as well as an array of motivational midlife transformations, *ROAR* is the closest thing to having Michael as a life coach—and an inspiring reminder that it is never too late to reinvent yourself."

—**Nina Garcia**, editor in chief of *Elle* magazine

"While reading Michael Clinton's sage advice along with the fascinating stories of people who ROARed into the second half of their life, you can't help but hear your own call to action. Each inspirational page engages your mind and soon you're chanting yes, yes, yes! A wonderfully written tutorial on how to squeeze the most juice out of every day from someone who has walked the walk. A must-read for anyone at any age."

—**McGarvey Black**, bestselling author of *Without Her Consent* and *The First Husband*

"Adventurer, marathoner, photographer, publisher, pilot, and author—Michael Clinton has spent his exuberant life pushing boundaries and reinventing himself. Based on his own experience as well as extensive interviews with friends and colleagues entering the next phase of life, *ROAR* is an inspirational and instructive look at how proactively plotting your future can make your second act as good, if not better, than your first."

—**Ann Lewnes**, chief marketing officer and executive vice president at Adobe

"A page-turner for anyone who has ever asked the question, 'Am I living my best, happiest life?'"

—**Alina Cho**, journalist

"This is a must-have guide for anyone who wants to be inspired about all the possibilities inherent in living one's best life."

—**Mary G. Berner**, president and CEO at Cumulus Media

"Michael Clinton's *Roar* is a candid owner's manual for the second part of life. With a robust framework for change, practical advice, and vibrant examples of men and women who have pivoted successfully, Clinton helps his readers exit the inertia of midlife and effect real change for enriched living."

—**Keith LaScalea, MD**

ROAR

into the second half
of your life
(*Before It's Too Late*)

MICHAEL CLINTON

ATRIA PAPERBACK
New York London Toronto Sydney New Delhi

BEYOND WORDS
Portland, Oregon

ATRIA PAPERBACK
A Division of Simon & Schuster, Inc.
1230 Avenue of the Americas
New York, NY 10020

BEYOND WORDS
1750 S.W. Skyline Blvd., Suite 20
Portland, Oregon 97221-2543
503-531-8700 / 503-531-8773 fax
www.beyondword.com

Managing Editor: Lindsay S. Easterbrooks-Brown
Editor: Emily Han
Copyeditor: Linda M. Meyer
Proofreader: Olivia Rollins
Design: Devon Smith
Composition: William H. Brunson Typography Services

First Beyond Words/Atria Paperback edition September 2022

10 9 8 7 6 5 4 3 2 1

Library of Congress Cataloging-in-Publication Data

Names: Clinton, Michael (Photographer), author.
Title: Roar : into the second half of your life (before it's too late) /
    Michael Clinton.
Description: First Beyond Words/Atria hardcover edition. | Portland, Oregon :
    Beyond Words, 2021. | Includes bibliographical references.
Identifiers: LCCN 2021014116 (print) | LCCN 2021014117 (ebook) | ISBN
    9781582708133 (hardcover) | ISBN 9781582708140 (paperback) | ISBN
    9781982165819 (ebook)
Subjects: LCSH: Self-actualization (Psychology) in middle age. | Middle
    age—Psychological aspects | Goal (Psychology)
Classification: LCC BF724.65.S44 C55 2021 (print) | LCC BF724.65.S44
    (ebook) | DDC 155.6/6—dc23
LC record available at https://lccn.loc.gov/2021014116
LC ebook record available at https://lccn.loc.gov/2021014117

The corporate mission of Beyond Words Publishing, Inc.: *Inspire to Integrity*

This book is dedicated to my father, Joseph,
who taught me about the marvels of the world and all of its possibilities.

Contents

Introduction

Making a major life change is hard. And it can be scary. But if you are stuck or trapped or unhappy, you have no choice but to change, since inaction may destroy you. In Buddhism, *bardo* is the state of existence between two lives—after one's death and before one's next rebirth. In this transitional state, to get to another place you have to let go of your current one. You don't really know where you will end up, but if you open yourself to the possibilities that are in front of you in all areas—from love to work to realizing the true you—you can successfully step into a new chapter of your life.

> *If you open yourself to the possibilities that are in front of you in all areas—from love to work to realizing the true you—you can successfully step into a new chapter of your life.*

When I first moved to New York from my native Pittsburgh, it was with $60, a college degree, a couch to sleep on for two months, and a dream to get into the magazine publishing business. I had no contacts—and in hindsight, no real clue—but I jumped in head-first. You might say that this is easy to do when you are twenty-two because you are a blank slate and willing to take risks, but I believe you can do this at any time in your life. In fact, sometimes you have to do it to move forward.

I did find my way (after some starts and stops and a recession thrown in) to a publishing career, starting at the bottom as a reporter for a business-to-business publication and working my way to the top of the industry as the president and publishing director of Hearst Magazines. At thirty-nine, I had an epiphany: I needed a lot more out of life. Thus, I created the concept of life layering and began my personal "ROAR into life" formula that I plan to use for the rest of my life. Throughout my journey, I realized that we have a lot of bandwidth, as long as we don't hinder our own possibilities! You'll learn about that and more as you read through this book.

Why Not You?

So many people I've talked to have no idea where they are going or want to go once they hit their mid-forties. They've lived an adult life for just over twenty years, and they wonder about some of their choices. Would they do it the same way if they could start over? My answer is to forget about what was, and start over now.

Those discussions are what led me to developing ROAR, a concept that is simple and understandable and can be followed by anyone if they adhere to these core principles. ROAR is an acronym that means to

REIMAGINE yourself
OWN who you are
ACT on what's next
REASSESS your relationships to get you there

The key question to ask yourself first is *Why not me?* Why shouldn't you be able to change your life? The short answer is that you can, and after reading this book, you will be inspired by real-life stories that show you how to do it.

With life expectancies getting longer for most people, you might have the opportunity to live multiple lives, from new careers to new loves to new passions. The traditional construct—marriage and a couple of kids, a job at a company for thirty years or more with a pension and a comfortable retirement—is being blown up every day. You may have lived that life once, but now there are "reimagineers" among us who are redefining what might be beyond the first half of one's life.

Now there are "reimagineers" among us who are redefining what might be beyond the first half of one's life.

You might have three different careers, not become a parent until you are fifty, or find a new love later in life. You might not blossom until you are in your sixties or seventies! Ignore all of those pundits who claim that as we age, we lose our capacity to create, to become entrepreneurs, to do daring things. I'm tired of hearing from psychologists and sociologists and any other "ists" who are constantly trying to limit who and what we might be over the span of a lifetime. Forget the words *age appropriate* and focus on *person appropriate*. Be the one who is seen as the role model for an engaged life.

While we're at it, let's banish the word *retire* and call it *refire* or *rewire* instead, as many people are living extraordinary lives after they leave their main professions. Let's stop cultural and self-imposed ageism too, and focus on self-imposed "growthism." It's time to purge many of the words that try to label us, as we gain years to our lives. In the second half of life, you can have a major renaissance in who you are and how you live.

Start that journey now.

Let's stop cultural and self-imposed ageism too, and focus on self-imposed "growthism."

It's Time to ROAR

The year 2020 was like no other in our lifetime. As the COVID-19 pandemic swept across the world, it upended our lives in ways we could have never imagined. Work changed, as did our personal goals and lifestyles, and relationships with our families, friends, and communities were uprooted. The Great Pause, as it has been called, has made us reflect and ask: *What is important in our lives? Are we on a path that will satisfy us individually? Do we have a lot of unlived moments that we pine for? Do we have a clear view of our future and what we truly want?*

ROAR was actually conceptualized before the pandemic, but as an idea it was never more relevant than in such fraught times, as so many of us began reassessing our lives and looking for inspiration from those who have successfully crossed over into a new second half.

In writing this book, I share the true stories of the more than forty individuals I interviewed, the majority being forty-five years old or older. Each one is a reimagineer, in that they completely changed their lives, in what I call a midlife awakening. Not a midlife crisis (which is an outdated idea) but an awakening: that as we get older, we gain the wisdom and hopefully the sense of urgency to make changes to our lives.

In June 2020, I commissioned the "'ROAR into the Second Half of Your Life' Survey" (conducted by Hudson Valley Insights and fielded by Qualtrics's Research-Services) to identify a nationally representative sample of adults between the ages of forty-five and seventy-five to gain insights into how people are thinking about their future aspirations and dreams. It also included some questions on how COVID-19 impacted their thinking or accelerated their decision to make a change. A total of 630 individuals responded—a cross-section of people from different walks of life, educational levels, marital statuses, ethnicities, and professions.[1]

Aging in combination with the pandemic has been a wake-up call for millions of people who have realized that they have got to move their lives forward—fast. What might have once been the luxury of time—to figure out what you will do next or how you really want to be spending your days—all of a sudden has taken on a sharper focus. A global virus forced us to confront it.

The message behind *ROAR* is that you need to put your life on hyperspeed until your dying breath, regardless of when that might be. You should run full gallop into your future, chasing everything that is important to you, ignoring what you are supposed to do or might do or should do. To have a second half of life that is overflowing with joy and satisfaction and fulfillment and purpose is the battle cry of this book.

The message behind ROAR *is that you need to put your life on hyperspeed until your dying breath, regardless of when that might be.*

It doesn't matter where you come from and what your life has been up to this point. You can find a new course, if you truly desire it. And sometimes it takes bold moves that are inspired by courageous thinking. To ROAR is to contradict and challenge all of what you thought about getting older, to have the imagination, the self-awareness, and the self-confidence to start anew. Your dreams are yours to make happen. It can start today. Ready. Set. Go. Let's ROAR!

PART I

Reimagine

Yourself

1

Reimagine Your Life before Others Do It for You

A bend in the road is not the end of the road
unless you fail to make the turn.
—Helen Keller

Face it, at some point you may no longer have your current job. You might be pushed out. Downsized. Aged out. Displaced. Replaced. It's increasingly likely that something is going to happen to radically change your work life, so why wait until that "something" happens to you? More than 40 million Americans experienced this as their lives were turned upside down during the COVID-19 pandemic. Some were hired back by their employers, but many found themselves laid off permanently, trying to figure out what to do next.

It's increasingly likely that something is going to happen to radically change your work life, so why wait until that "something" happens to you?

The same thing can happen in your personal life. What if you have been struggling in a relationship that once seemed rock-solid? You might be subconsciously ignoring the signals that your differences have become irreconcilable, and you are shocked when your partner informs you that they want to leave. You're being pushed out in a personal way, perhaps being replaced by someone new. In the panic of the moment, you wonder what will happen to you. On the other hand, if the relationship was never on sound footing, you must have thought about what you would do if things fell apart. Or maybe not; denial is a potent emotion!

Other things can happen to you, too. An illness. A natural disaster. Have you thought about what your plan would be if you became seriously ill? Or if you were forced to leave your home or town, as thousands of people did when Katrina hit New Orleans? When COVID-19 swept across the world, it forced countless people to rethink not only *how* they would live but also *where* they would live and what they wanted in their lives moving forward. The prospect of being a victim was a wake-up call for millions of people, who realized that a virus could take them down at any time.

ROAR TIP

We need to be in a constant state of reimagining, thinking through the next phase of every aspect of our lives. You can start that process at any time, if you are committed to true change. Why not reimagine yourself before someone or something "reimagines" your life for you?

Major life change is not easy. Most of us put it off because it is hard work. We don't want to think about the possibility of losing a job or a spouse or a way of life, yet we know when the signals are there. Why not be proactive in moving forward with your life before it's too late?

If you are in mid-career, now is the time to ask yourself if you are doing what you want to do and if you will be happy doing it for the next twenty years. If you are leaving a career or retiring from your current job, have you thought through a plan for the next twenty years or more? In both cases, saying that you will figure it out when you get there just isn't going to work. In this book, you'll hear many stories of people who have successfully pivoted to a new place. Some have done it once, and others are serial reimagineers!

Now is the time to ask yourself if you are doing what you want to do and if you will be happy doing it for the next twenty years.

I spoke with a longtime teacher[1] who regretted that she didn't know what to do with herself once she decided to retire.

"I'm driving my husband crazy," she said, laughing. "I need to figure something out." Too many people find themselves in that place.

Many people in my industry were displaced before they wanted to leave. The magazine industry, like newspapers and now television, has undergone tremendous transformation in the past twenty years. Numerous editors and publishers were pushed out in their forties and fifties, never to find jobs in their industry again. Many have floundered, some while trying their luck at selling real estate or attempting to create consulting gigs in the industry.

Some have proactively reimagined their lives, like my friend Polly,[2] who was a journalist for a major metropolitan newspaper in the Southwest. At fifty-two and as a divorced mother of one daughter, she dreamed about a different future. She tried to ignore the thoughts, but as she moved farther into her fifties, she thought about her cousin who had reimagined herself.

"If I don't do it at fifty-five, I won't do it at sixty-five," her cousin had told Polly, announcing that she was going to sell her commercial silk screen business and her home in the Northwest and move to Santa Barbara, where she had grown up, to become a full-time painter. Polly's cousin said she figured that if she didn't sell anything in the first year, she could always get a job at a gallery. Within the first three months, she sold three paintings and her new career was launched.

Polly wasn't exactly sure what she wanted to do, but she decided to take it step by step. For starters, she knew she needed to save money. She sold her house and about half of her belongings and moved in with a roommate. She asked herself some tough questions about what she found meaningful and motivating. She had always had an interest in depth psychology (the science of the unconscious), so when she heard about a master's degree program at Pacifica Graduate Institute in California—to which one could commute once a month for three-day intensives—she was intrigued. At fifty-five, after twenty years of working for a newspaper (that was then going through layoffs), she decided it was time to quit her job and move forward in her life.

She learned that if she were to pursue the graduate degree, she would need to use the profits from selling her house. Her financial planner said to her at the time, "Don't do it; you really can't afford it. But," he continued, "as your friend, I would tell you that you have to do it." And so, Polly made the leap, commuting and studying to become a licensed therapist. Today, she works in public health, within the opioid crisis, and feels fulfilled in her new career. She met a man and is remarried, thriving in her mid-sixties, loving her new life.

"My financial planner was right. I couldn't really afford this path, but the good thing is that therapists can work into their eighties and nineties, and if you love the work, then it doesn't seem like work. The way I look at it now is that I couldn't afford not to take this path," she said.

ROAR TIP

Use your network to help you pivot. You know more people than you think you do. Everyone is a possible connection to a next step. Take time to regularly go through your contacts, organizing them and even adding notes about their various professions and associations. Make a point when meeting new people—whether professionally or socially—to follow your intuition if you sense a connection with someone, and ask to exchange contact information. You just never know!

Dawn Steele Halbert[3] was another casualty of the disrupted publishing industry, when she was laid off at fifty-nine from the magazine company she had worked at for twelve years. After a thirty-year career with stints at *Essence*, *Ebony*, and other magazines, she was forced to pivot. Tapping into her network, she first started working with a partner who created the I Am That Woman Retreat, which focuses on Black professional women in the later stages of their careers, about to be empty nesters, or looking for their next opportunity. Dawn, too, made an entrepreneurial discovery, when she joined a life insurance company called Symmetry Financial Group.

The company allows her to have real and meaningful conversations with people about their circumstances. Bringing solutions to their lives is now the course that she is on. At sixty-three, in her native Chicago, she is focusing on financial literacy education and protection for the African American community. A successful pivot from a corporate job to an entrepreneurial business has given her purpose for the future.

If Polly's and Dawn's industries hadn't been disrupted with heavy layoffs, these individuals might not have thought about their own future directions. Fortunately, they were proactive in regrouping.

There are countless stories of midlife individuals who have made huge moves. Colonel Sanders didn't franchise his secret recipe until he was sixty-two.[4] Ray Kroc founded McDonald's when he was fifty-two,[5] and Leo Goodwin was fifty when he and his wife Lillian launched Geico.[6] But you don't have to be a household name to make your mark. According to an article in *Entrepreneur*, Jim Butenschoen left the IT business at sixty-five and created the Career Academy for Hair Design in Arkansas.[7] Dave Bateman, a Washington State lawyer, and his wife Trudy, an emergency room nurse, fell in love with the idea of becoming coffee growers in Kona, Hawaii. When they were both in their late fifties, they launched Heavenly Hawaiian Farms, where they produce and distribute their own blend of coffee, a move that Bateman says is "not retirement, but a change of focus. A change of life."[8] And Gerry Fioriglio started the Family Caregivers Network at fifty-seven in her native Pennsylvania.[9]

What drove all these midlifers to ROAR into their second half? A vision. A passion. A desire to create something that was fulfilling to them.

ROAR TIP

Learning new skills is possible at any age and can lead to new directions and opportunities. *What is your passion? What skills are you interested in acquiring? What might be some of the tools you can use to start reimagining the new you, and how can you learn about and gain access to them?*

Change is everywhere you look. Countless brick-and-mortar retail businesses are shutting down because of the rapid rise of online shopping.

The pandemic hastened the demise of many stores, from the closure of Pier One and Tuesday Morning to the bankruptcy of Neiman Marcus and JCPenney. Transportation has changed with the advent of ride services such as Uber and Lyft. The medical industry, too, is changing, with more people visiting urgent-care locations than general practice doctors, and fitness centers being replaced by online training.

If you are in an industry that is challenged, you don't necessarily have to leave it, but you do need to reimagine yourself and your skill set. In the disruption of the publishing business, I watched print-skilled individuals learn new skills for the digital age. Todd, for example, jumped in headfirst to learn the digital world and became a highly successful sales executive in that area, giving him a lot more latitude for future moves.

I turned to my friend Julianna Margulies,[10] the award-winning actress you might know from *ER* and her seven-year run as Alicia Florrick in *The Good Wife*. As someone who is constantly reimagining a new character, she had some helpful insights. In order to understand how her lawyer character thinks and acts, she studied lawyers' behavior.

"My grandmother, Henrietta Greenspan, was one of the first women to graduate from New York University Law School, so I spent a lot of time researching her life along with the history of other women lawyers. I wanted to understand their journey and absorb it into my skin. Also, my husband is a lawyer by training, so he was able to help me have a deeper understanding of how a lawyer thinks," she told me. One of the lessons she learned by acting the part of a lawyer was to stand back and watch both sides of an argument before making any type of judgment. While that isn't her natural behavior, doing so helped her see how effective a lawyer could be with that skill.

When Julianna was preparing for her role on *ER*, she went to a Cook County hospital in Chicago and was allowed to trail the nurses in the emergency room. She explained that until you walk in someone's shoes, you can't have a perspective. You need to be in the room with them.

In her book *Sunshine Girl: An Unexpected Life*, Julianna talks about taking on new roles and a lot more—lessons for anyone who is thinking about exploring different roles in life.

Even if you are the star or your name is on the door, you're not exempt. Designer Donna Karan stepped down from her eponymous company, but she didn't let that stop her from reimagining herself. After she sold her company to luxury-goods giant LVMH (Moët Hennessy Louis Vuitton) at fifty-nine, she started Urban Zen, a philosophy of living inspired by world cultures. Balancing philanthropy and commerce, she sells clothing, home accessories, and jewelry, but her latest business endeavor is a whole lot more. It promotes holistic wellness, children's education, and integrative training. While she may have stepped into the reimagineering process, today, in her early seventies, Donna is thriving. She has far surpassed peers who were forced out of business and are not even close to living such a dynamic and fulfilled life.[11]

You might say that Donna had lots of resources to start her own business, but I assure you that anybody can find their own solution, given a strong drive to succeed. One of my favorite examples is my friend Maggie Lentz,[12] whom I met at the Berlin Marathon. The moment we met, she had a sparkle, an aura around her that told me that she was very special. She is one of the lucky ones, having realized early (as she approached her fortieth birthday) that she needed to reimagine herself.

A married mother of three living in Houston, Maggie is an Ecuadorean native who came to the US for college, became an American citizen, and stayed. She was an award-winning teacher in her district, as well as bilingual teacher of the year, but she felt that something was missing.

"I kept saying to myself, *There must be something more out there*," she said. "Also, I wanted more freedom and the ability to make more money for my family. I started reading about other things that might appeal to me. One thing I knew is that I wanted to be of service to people." When she was in her twenties, Maggie dealt with cervical cancer on her own in America, while her family was in Ecuador. That, coupled with her father's death the same year, had a huge influence on her. She isn't wasting any more time.

Ultimately, Maggie recognized her true entrepreneurial spirit and started a company called Hello Freedom. She focused on health coaching and obtained a certificate to become a running coach. She manages a friend's health and wellness company that leads a group of trainers who bring family and kids' workouts to your home. She also finds time to be an ambassador for a group that sponsors Go Run for Fun initiatives and races against violence, as well as other business activities.

"I'm in charge of my own destiny; it's creative and fast-changing, and I'm thriving," explained Maggie, who also focuses on her own fitness, with fifteen marathons under her belt. She plans to spend the rest of her life focused on ways to bring health and fitness to people, as her lifestyle and her profession.

> **ROAR TIP**
>
> Think back to your childhood dreams, and pursue what you dreamed about. It's still inside your brain, you just need to bring it front and center again. Once you have it, hold on to it—then work at reviving it.

Sometimes life can hit you with a triple whammy, as it did with Jim Gath,[13] a highly successful marketing executive who worked for major companies and started his own business in the entertainment and hospitality industry. At fifty he was forced to close the business: the economy was in a downturn, his wife left him, and he realized he needed to go into rehab for alcoholism. "I went out into a field and sat under a tree and said, *I have nothing. For the first time in my life, I can do anything that I want to do,*" he explained.

As a way to start his new life, Jim acknowledged that hanging out with horses was something he had always loved. He searched the internet and found a job as a wrangler at a kids' camp in Malibu, which led to working at the Los Angeles Equestrian Center. He saved some money to buy two horses and then got a third, offering riding lessons. A friend owned a horse-rescue ranch in Arizona, and he moved there, thinking that he might even open his own boarding facility.

When his mother inherited some money, she and his sister joined Jim in funding what is now the Tierra Madre Horse & Human Sanctuary in Cave Creek, Arizona. They provide a forever home for more than twenty-five neglected, abandoned, and abused horses. In return, they help children and adults who need therapeutic support in a safe space. A 501(c)(3), Tierra Madre relies on support from the community, and as Jim said, it was tough going in the beginning. Jim said he spent fifty years looking for something he didn't know he was looking for. "I chased material happiness, and I was empty inside. I feel like I've found a place in the world, to make it a little better every day, make a kid smile, make a horse feel a little better. It is all where God lives."

Jim lives in a small apartment right in the barn. He remembers his big house and fancy car, but he believes that God will provide you with what you need, though maybe not everything you want. But pretty soon, you will come to the realization that having everything you need is all you really want. From a moment of being lost, Jim, now sixty-nine, has found true purpose in life through his love of horses.

I interviewed over forty people like Jim, who have successfully reimagined their lives. I met Paul Pakusch, who found happiness driving a school bus, and Jeanne Marin, a dermatologist who went back to school at fifty-five to become a veterinarian. (You'll hear more about Paul and Jeanne in chapter 6, "Own Your Losses, Weaknesses, Failures, and Threats.") Fatima Latief Soeryonegoro[14] also successfully reinvented herself.

Fatima was born in the Indonesian city of Manado but for the past eleven years has been a resident of Sydney, Australia, with her American-born husband and two sons. When they moved from Jakarta to Sydney, she left her sales-and-marketing career in the retail and hospitality world to raise her kids full-time. In her early fifties, Fatima realized it was time to think about her own next chapter.

Fashion had always been a passion of hers, influenced by her mother, who was a designer in the early 1960s. After enrolling in the Australian Style Institute in Melbourne, Fatima learned about personal and commercial styling, as well as corporate and image consulting in the world of fashion. She ultimately started her own business as a stylist. Her collaboration with public relations firms, photographers, and modeling agencies led to working on fashion editorials for magazines, taking on private clients, and more. Despite embarking on this new career—from scratch—in her mid-fifties, Fatima has been able to carve out a reputation for her skills in Australia, along with a promising future on the global fashion scene. While fashion was always a major interest, it wasn't until she decided to pursue it as a second-half-of-life profession that it became a dream come true. With her kids grown up and her husband supporting her every step of the way, Fatima's business is thriving!

Helen Appleyard,[15] a native of Perth, Australia, was burned out from work and a broken relationship at forty-five years old. A divorced mother of one daughter, she had worked as a state manager for a global liquor company. She took a trip to Italy to decompress and to focus on mindfulness, meditation, and reading books about Buddhism, as a way to find her purpose.

Upon her return to Australia, meditation and yoga became integral to Helen's life. She met a new man, remarried, and decided it was time to build a life of giving back. She started small by helping to raise money for the purchase of iPads designed specifically for severely disabled students. This led to working with other charities in Western Australia, and then with Street Friends, an organization in which she has made a major impact on alleviating homelessness in Perth. She helped this organization build on its mission, in part by raising money to rent a home where food could be prepared, items stored, and the clothes of homeless people washed.

Simultaneously, Helen trained to teach meditation, and in 2018 she started Shine Meditation WA. Her practice includes individuals, schools, and corporations, and as she said, her mission is to help people "find the gold from within them." She works with children who are experiencing stress and anxiety at young ages, watching them grow through mindfulness.

In early 2020, Helen decided it was time to take another step. She began a course at the Australian Institute of Professional Counsellors, and in 2022, at sixty, she will become a qualified counselor, combining meditation and a counseling practice. "I now have a purpose and a vision for my life, bringing a level of nonsecular spirituality into my work. I have never been happier or truer. It took a while, but I now know myself and what I'm meant to do."

Regardless of where you are in your life, you will be inspired by the stories of the people I talked to in writing *ROAR*. Somewhere in these examples, you'll find your own *aha* moment that will let you get unstuck and move to a better and happier future. Of course, with change comes risk. Some people might fail in their first attempt, but they will have learned the important lesson that if they try and don't succeed, they can always try again—as well as be surprised by what they have learned in the process.

> *In this book, I hope to offer insights and tools that you too can use to ROAR into the second half of your life.*

In this book, I hope to offer insights and tools that you too can use to ROAR into the second half of your life. If you are in your fifties, you are already getting the sense that life moves fast. If you are in your sixties or older, that sense is amplified, and you are realizing that there is a finite amount of time to accomplish what your life legacy will be. You can lament that, or you can spring forward into an action plan, before it is too late!

These four steps of ROAR—REIMAGINE yourself, OWN who you are, ACT on what's next, and REASSESS your relationships to get you there—are the process to get you to your next life stage, filled with satisfaction, fulfillment, and joy.

ROAR: Chapter Takeaways

With all the reimagineers whom I talked to, there were a few recurring themes that emerged, lessons and questions for everyone who is contemplating a change:

- Be true to yourself. It is time to throw off self-imposed restrictions, as well as those placed on you by your spouse, your family, or your community. Are you being true to yourself? What kinds of restrictions are holding you back? Spend time reflecting and journaling your thoughts. Make a list of all the things that are preventing you from living an authentic life. Getting clear and being honest is a powerful first step to change.
- Time is running out. If you don't do it now, you will stay in the same rut and be stuck in an unhappy place. Are you ready to become a reimagineer? Start by envisioning what a reimagineer is to you. Are there people you admire who are reimagineer role models? Look to them for inspiration and ideas.

- It takes time. Most everyone who pivots has thought it through over a one-to-two-year period before starting the journey. Can you make that commitment? Write that commitment into a personal mission statement and put it somewhere so you see it every day.
- Personal passion is a powerful motivator for fulfillment, whether you find it in your work or what you need in a relationship or in the place where you live. What brings you joy? Think back on your childhood dreams and ambitions. Write them down. Is there one that speaks to your heart right now?
- The most successful people who have created change in midlife have an insatiable curiosity about the world and are lifelong learners. Make a list of what you are curious about, and then check out your local library or community college and the internet for more information on how you can learn more.

2

Reimagine Your Favorite Future—
Then Live It

*The important thing to you is not how many years in your life, but
how much life in your years!*
—Edward J. Stieglitz, *The Second Forty Years*

I hate the word *retire*. It's one of those toxic words that makes it sound like
you are going to check out of life. It conjures up images of woeful, gray-
haired people pulling back from life in a way that gives me the creeps! The
notion that someone should ride off into the sunset with the proverbial
gold watch and spend the rest of their days in some state of suspension
needs to be blown up. My friend Lynne came up with a new word. She
calls it her "refire" period, a time when she is pursuing everything on her
life list—and she's doing it with a vengeance, starting with a trip around
the world. Others call it a "rewire," where they start pursuits that are very
different from those in the first half of their lives.

There are 83 million Americans between the ages of forty-five and
sixty-four, and 103 million between forty and sixty-four, comprising 41
percent of all US adults.[1] Many of them are going to redefine getting
older in amazing ways. It's already happening, and you can be among
them. Why not start a whole new career at fifty or sixty or seventy? The
idea that we should step out of our main career and never start over
again is a ridiculous notion.

Yes, there are still many people in their sixties and seventies who continue to work in their main profession, whether it is the accomplished

actress Helen Mirren at seventy-six or longtime politician Joe Biden, who became president of the United States at seventy-eight. Dr. Anthony Fauci, who turned eighty in 2020, played a critical role in how we dealt with the COVID pandemic, and then there are professors like Robert J. Nash, who is just hitting eighty and has written about celebrating, not retiring from, his teaching post at the University of Vermont.[2] If your idea of your favorite future is to work in your profession for as long as you'd like, I say go for it. Just look at Mick Jagger, still rocking in his seventies!

The idea that we should step out of our main career and never start over again is a ridiculous notion.

Sometimes what might be called a "re-career" can take on an interesting twist, as in the case of Gayle King,[3] who returned to being a daily television anchor after many years of not being on the air with that kind of regularity. She has a long history of local television broadcasting in cities like Baltimore (where she met her best friend, Oprah Winfrey), Kansas City, and Hartford (where she spent eighteen years as the key anchor). Gayle made a big splash on national television when she joined *CBS Morning News* as coanchor in 2012 at the age of fifty-seven, and when she became the lead anchor in 2019, at sixty-four! A role model for many women in broadcasting who have been victims of ageism, Gayle continues to be at the top of her game. I got to know Gayle when she joined the team of *O, The Oprah Magazine* as editor-at-large, and I was always in awe of how she was able to accomplish so much in a given day. She still has many chapters of her storied career ahead of her.

However, some people are happy to wrap up a career and start a brand-new pursuit, whether by design or by an opportunity that presents itself.

Jack Kliger[4] is a great example. At seventy-one, he became the president and CEO of the Museum of Jewish Heritage in New York City. While he had been on that board for many years, he never thought about actually running the museum, the third-largest of its kind in the world after Yad Vashem in Israel and the United States Holocaust Memorial Museum in Washington, DC.

As the son of survivors of the Budapest and Polish ghettos, Jack explained that a lot of the children of the "second generation" did not necessarily grow up with a lot of conversation about the horrors of what happened. His father was able to escape into the woods outside the town of Lutsk, Poland, just before twenty-five thousand Jews were killed by the Nazis, a story that Jack learned about when he was twelve years old.

It wasn't until his only daughter's bat mitzvah, when he saw a picture of his fourteen-year-old mother in the Budapest ghetto and wearing the yellow star on her jacket, that he realized his daughter looked just like her. His mother had been robbed of her teenage life, and he knew he needed to take part in making sure this would never happen again to other children. He got involved in the Museum of Jewish Heritage, an institution that focuses on remembrance, education, and renewal. "I get the opportunity to benefit survivors, their grandchildren, and people in general to understand what happened and that with the trauma of loss, there is hope and can be renewal after a dark period," he told me.

His long-running successful business career behind him, Jack has launched a new career and is on a journey of renewal himself, one that is not only deeply personal but also rich with meaning and purpose. I'd call that a refire.

Susan Black[5] is another great example of refiring. Susan is one of a new breed of older entrepreneurs who are starting businesses that create services for seniors. Many of the ideas have a low cost of entry, including becoming a "senior manager," where you take on clients and help them with financial management, healthcare requirements, and everyday needs like shopping for food. Or you might take courses that teach you about stretching and low-impact exercises and turn that into a business to help seniors maintain balance and flexibility.

Susan worked for over forty years in the travel and hospitality industry. She traveled the world on behalf of her clients, as she and her husband raised two children, now adults in their twenties. Her new journey started when she was sixty-one years old and lost her best friend to cancer. Thinking about her own health, she had to face the fact that she had gained over one hundred pounds and was filled with stress. She realized that she had to quit her job to seriously focus on self-care and self-worth. Over ten months, she reduced her weight from

240 to 140 pounds, through an emphasis on hiking and an improved eating regimen. With encouragement from her family and her ninety-five-year-old mother, who lives in assisted living, Susan was able to create a healthier self.

As she thought about her next chapter, the COVID-19 crisis hit, and her attention turned to her mother, who all of a sudden found herself in lockdown with the many other seniors in her facility. Susan talked to her on the phone with an occasional "window visit." During one of the calls, her mother—an early trailblazer, earning an MBA in the 1940s—complained that the social isolation and lack of relevant activities were detrimental to so many seniors. And it was now compounded by the lockdown. "My mother was never interested in bingo or flower arranging, which is what was being offered," explained Susan.

It led to an idea. Together, they would create a platform of what they called content and conversation that could be delivered to individuals on a laptop via Zoom technology. They started with a collection of programs that included mindfulness and gratitude but evolved into issues such as love and marriage. It was an instant hit during a time when so many were feeling isolated. Sensing a bigger opportunity, Susan and her mother established Wowzitude, designed to put a "wow" in your day and to combine attitude and gratitude as the underlying mission.

As the word got out via local media, more long-term-care facilities reached out, asking if they could tap into the programming, particularly as the offerings grew to over one hundred unique one-hour topics that helped seniors engage with each other, even though they were not able to be together physically. Wowzitude continued to grow. Sadly, though, Susan's mother contracted the COVID-19 virus and, at the age of ninety-seven, died in July 2020.

Susan realized that she had found her calling. She knew that Wowzitude would not only be a legacy of her mother's life but also would serve so many other mothers (and fathers) by keeping them engaged and current and conversing with each other. Wowzitude is now in fourteen markets via a subscription model. Individuals, companies, and foundations have expressed an interest in helping to fund the initiative, and Susan is ROARing in a direction she had never even thought about until she realized that there was a need. When I asked her about her start-up costs, she explained that it took little more than a Zoom account, some innovative ideas, and some experience with PowerPoint, graphics, and video.

According to a study by the Ewing Marion Kauffman Foundation in 2019, nearly 25 percent of new entrepreneurs were between fifty-five and sixty-four, almost double from twenty years prior.[6] When I spoke to Sameeksha Desai, director of research at the Kauffman Foundation, she explained to me that seniors can engage in entrepreneurial activities without starting a business. The research shows that about six in ten people sixty-five and up who are starting a business or starting to work for themselves said that they wanted appreciable financial means—and to follow a passion.[7] By exploring technology platforms such as Rover (to become a dog walker), TaskRabbit (to become a tasker in a variety of areas), or Upwork (which connects businesses of all sizes to freelancers and independent professionals), anyone can engage in some type of entrepreneurial work, be their own boss, and have more independence.

ROAR TIP

Whether you want to participate in an entrepreneurial activity or start one of your own, technology has become a great enabler to get you launched. A resource to delve deeper into the topic is *Hustle and Gig: Struggling and Surviving in the Sharing Economy*, a book by Alexandrea J. Ravenelle.

With people living longer lives, there will be numerous emerging needs for serving what is going to become a major transformation of society with a growing older population. This will start with the boomer generation, as life expectancies continue to expand based on health breakthroughs and preventative medicine. In his book *Gray Dawn: How the Coming Age Wave Will Transform America—and the World*, author and prominent businessman Peter G. Peterson gives a futuristic view of what it will mean to have large groups of people who are sixty-five and over living productive and interesting lives. We will need a new word for this emerging group, as *elderly* and other old-fashioned terms just aren't going to cut it anymore.

The aforementioned Susan Black, now sixty-three years old, understands what might be needed to come up with a business idea and serve this emerging "gray" population. "Anyone can start an idea, if they identify a need," she explained. By tapping into skills honed from decades in her own business career, Susan has become one of the innovative entrepreneurs driving fresh ideas into the culture by addressing the needs of a different kind of person who will live into their nineties and beyond.

Nadine Karp McHugh[8] is a highly respected global media director for major companies such as Colgate and L'Oréal. Even though she saw success in her own career, in her early fifties Nadine began to see more and more inequality between men and women—not only in the workforce but also in American culture in general. She concentrated on how she might be able to help: by working as a volunteer with trade organizations and joining the board of the Association of National Advertisers (ANA).

In 2016, the group started a separate operating division of the ANA, with a mission to drive the accurate portrayal of women and girls in marketing, advertising, media, and entertainment, so girls can see themselves as they truly are—and see all of their potential. As the group says, "If you can see her, you can be her." They also created GEM— Gender Equality Measurement—to show how having more positive portrayals of women is good for business, as well as society at large. It was an epiphany for Nadine. She grew further engaged and was asked to become the first president of this new operating division of the ANA.

"I had wanted to create more impact, to make a difference in my everyday working life," Nadine said. "SeeHer was one of those defining moments. It feeds my soul and moves me forward as a person. I came from a humble background, and now my focus is on how I can help my daughter's generation and her daughter's generation have better lives." An opportunity appeared that allowed her to move into her own favorite future.

While Nadine is running this group, I would urge the ANA to start a similar initiative that shows people over fifty in a more positive way. If you see them, you can be them!

Anyone can make a change if they desire it. Jeanine Lombardi[9] had met Chris through their kids and their sports programs. While in their mid-forties, she worked as a general manager for a restaurant chain and Chris worked in construction, as they raised their five kids from both marriages. As Jeanine liked to say, she had three biological children, her first at seventeen, and two bonus children, who were Chris's kids.

They both wanted a change in their lives and one day decided to move to North Carolina, where two of their kids lived. "I wanted a shift in life, something a little calmer, and my husband was beginning to feel the effects of years of construction work," she said.

When they arrived in their new city, Charlotte, North Carolina, Jeanine jumped back into restaurant work but soon learned that their life was just as busy and crazy as when they lived in the Northeast. "Working with young adults all the time is like being a referee, and I was getting weary of people complaining that their steak wasn't good enough. I wanted to do something more worthwhile," she explained.

When COVID-19 put her out of work, she started taking online courses from the local community college. She studied medical terminology and took pharmacy technician classes (she's now certified) and Nurse's Aide 1, an introductory course offered by a private nursing institution. "I realized that I wanted to work at something that allowed me to sit with a patient and make them feel better, and being a nurse's aide was where I could do that," she said, adding that she was now taking the second course for the program.

Jeanine is now on a path that will evolve over time, but the important thing is that she found the way that will lead her into a more fulfilling future. As for Chris, he is now the manager of an auto mechanic store, working sane hours and being off on weekends. It has given him respite from the backbreaking work of construction.

ROAR TIP

We can't always control our outer circumstances, but what we can control is ourselves—how we respond, the decisions we make, and how we plan for our future. Take time to plan your future and get clear about your specific goals. Write them down and look at them every day, letting them guide your steps toward realizing the future you want!

After forty-two years in the publishing business, I was ready for a personal pivot. I had had a splendid career, reaching the top of my profession as president and publishing director of Hearst Magazines. I had the honor of being on the team that launched *O, The Oprah Magazine* and partnerships with Food Network and HGTV, as well as publishing twenty other magazines, including *Esquire* and *Harper's Bazaar*.

Our team had bought two publishing companies, becoming the largest global magazine company in the world. It had been my honor to serve as the chairman of Magazine Publishers of America, our leading trade organization, as well as to be recognized as one of the industry leaders by several business-to-business journals. I had also been named to the Board of Directors of the Hearst Corporation, thanks to our executive vice chairman and former CEO, Frank Bennack, one of my valued mentors.

For a kid who had arrived in New York City with no contacts, I had achieved career success beyond my wildest dreams. But all my life I had admired people who had the courage to step out while they were on top or to "take themselves out" when the time was right. It was always my goal to be one of them, and over time, I realized I was ready to take that step.

ROAR TIP

When the day arrives to take your next step, my best advice is for you to take control of your own narrative and repeat it over and over again. And be prepared to talk about what you are going to do next. It's fine to say, "I'm spending more time with my family and my hobbies," but you need a better plan. You need to map out that future.

While I was formulating my plan, I grappled with the word *retire*. I had a very specific plan about what I was going to do next, and the word *retire* sounded so final! Plus, in the media business when you say that you are going to retire, everyone starts gossiping about whether you are being pushed out! As I said to a colleague, "We are all entitled to close out a career and be proactive about our timing on our own terms."

My narrative was that I had a phenomenal forty-two-year run and loved every minute of it, but I was ready for a new adventure that included a well-thought-out list of what I was going to do next. I had spent nearly two years thinking about it, and when the time was right, I was locked and loaded. My plan was to start a second master's degree at Columbia University, focusing on the nonprofit world and philanthropy, a topic that was near to my heart, as I serve on many boards and had started my own foundation (which I'll discuss in chapter 12, "Reassess Your Community and Your Relationship with It"). This book was on my mind, as was adding to my country count in my travels (already 124), building on my fifteen marathon runs, and more.

The response was phenomenal. Colleagues, clients, and fellow industry executives were generous in their response and support, while many of them told me they hoped that they would have their next step so well planned out. It leads to the question: *What's your favorite future?*

I first heard those words from David Verklin,[10] who was a longtime client and business leader. David and I were both from Pittsburgh, and we bonded when we met in our early thirties. He had been a wunderkind in the ad agency business, ultimately becoming the CEO of one of the largest media agencies in the US.

He would often pose that question to companies and to individuals, making them think about their goals. Over the years, I would always ask him, "David, what's your favorite future?" and we would exchange thoughts about what we each wanted in our lives beyond our careers.

ROAR TIP

One of the greatest exercises is to ask yourself these questions: *Am I happy with my life right now? Or am I just dreaming of my "unlived life"? Is there something I want to do that I haven't done? Am I living someone else's dream and not my own?* Reflect on your answers, and identify what area in your life needs your attention.

When Rob Smith[11] was a young man growing up in Michigan, he had a sincere desire to be a social worker, with an emphasis on helping underrepresented people. At the time, his father said that if Rob followed that course, then he wouldn't pay for college, so Rob focused on business instead. In addition, as he explained, he "manifested" the kind of person his family wanted him to be: a football player and one of the cool kids in college. He went on to spend thirty years as a retail executive in Florida and New York before he had his own moment of awakening.

"I decided that I needed to go on a journey to see who I was and what I wanted to do with my life," he said. He went to a wellness center and to Burning Man, an annual event in the desert of Nevada—which is an experiment in community and art influenced by ten principles, including communal effort and radical self-expression. Those experiences, when he was fifty, made him realize that he needed a major change. He gave five months' notice at work, saved as much money as he could, and went on a six-month trip to study ancient cultures, civilizations, and religion.

Along the way, he thought about entering politics, doing public service, becoming an executive director of a nonprofit. In Peru, he participated in an ayahuasca ceremony, where he drank the ayahuasca brew made from local vines, plants, and other ingredients. This hallucinogenic beverage is viewed as sacred by some and results in a psychedelic experience. Under its spell, he had the revelation that he needed to get back to his roots in focusing on social justice. "I was sitting naked on a rock and met myself as a boy and said, *I'm so sorry that I left you behind.*" It was the epiphany that created the ROAR into his future.

Rob had always been interested in gender identity, and now that it was a major topic emerging in society, he wanted to spend his time exploring that. The idea for what became the Phluid Project came to him that night in Peru. He would create a safe space for young people, accepting everyone who felt they were different.

With a mission to challenge boundaries with humanity and values centered on acceptance, balance, integrity, and openness, the project became a life space in Soho in New York with gender-free clothing, seminars, and a place for activism and social justice. Rob said that he had to educate himself on what was happening in this sphere, as he built a business that included gender-expansive training and consulting for companies.

"It became a drive that I can't explain," he said, while admitting that he burned through most of his savings to make the project happen. But at fifty-five, Rob is now committed to teaching and awakening people to open their hearts and minds, in an effort to advocate for all who are underrepresented. His next goal is to become an advocate and work on behalf of disabled people in our culture.

Rob found his favorite future by reclaiming a boyhood dream. It may have taken him several decades to get there, but he is now embracing his true self as he progresses into the future.

ROAR TIP

Don't wait for a crisis to show you your path. Now is the time to ask: *What do I want my future to look like?* One way to "see" your future is to create a vision board by collecting images and words that represent the future you want, such as how or where you would like to live. The key is to use images that depict as clearly as possible what it is you want, and how you want to feel as your future self. Lastly, spend time with your vision board every day. For more information, search "vision board" online or see this book's Recommended Resources section.

If you were suddenly diagnosed with a serious illness, it would put your life into perspective pretty quickly. Jonathan,[12] a senior executive at a global lifestyle brand, was forty-three years old, married, and the father of three small children when his doctor called him during his morning commute. "I had been to my daughter's dance recital that morning, so I was running a bit late for work. All I can remember is that he said 'leukemia,' and that he needed me to go to the hospital that day," he said.

It was a Friday and on Monday, he was hospitalized for what would be twelve weeks with a few intermittent home stays, as he was treated with chemotherapy. For three weeks at a time, he wasn't able to see his children and thought he was going to die, as he battled acute myeloid leukemia. "I'm British, so 'keep calm and carry on' is one of our mottos, but it was awful, so hard to describe. I had to decide to spend all of my time not thinking about the medical stats or my odds, but rather shift into a powerful place of optimism and positivity," he explained.

His wife, a natural optimist, played a significant role during his hours of treatment, as they pondered their future, always focusing on a good result. Ultimately, the diagnosis made Jonathan and his wife think about everything. Should they stay in New York? Should he stay in his high-stress, demanding job? What should be the future of their family?

"You can't know what your favorite future will be unless you really reassess your life and do it at full bore," he said, something that he was forced to do as a byproduct of his diagnosis. It also required him doing a lot of work with himself, including some therapy so that he could have more clarity about what he should do moving forward. As his doctor said to him, it's the terrible things in life that make people reassess. "I would take a walk into Central Park and sit and watch some kids play ball and wonder if I should become an athletics teacher, since I was always interested in all kinds of sports," he said.

Jonathan became very aware that time is finite, asking himself a question that usually has more urgency for someone much older than him: *What does time need to give me and what do I want to put into it?* As he searched his soul, he realized that his dream to come to New York with his young family was the right one, giving them an experience that would shape their lives. He decided to stay with his job, since he loved what he did and the people he did it with. "My management was incredibly supportive, keeping my job open and making it easy for me to re-transition on my own terms. That counts."

Today, three years later, Jonathan is happy and healthy. In his case, he had to go deep into himself to come to the conclusion that he should stay the course for now. His family is thriving, and he continues to be one of the top people in his field. "I didn't believe that the sky could fall on my head, but it did," he said, explaining that he is more open in general, spends precious time with his kids, and definitely does not let the small stuff get in the way.

As the expression goes, the only way out is to go in. That's what Jonathan did, finding that his favorite future had been the course he was on, but he needed to turn it inside out before he could move forward. In his mid-forties, Jonathan experienced something that many people face when they are decades older. He'll take this lesson with him for the rest of his life, letting him ROAR into his fifties and beyond.

> ## ROAR TIP
>
> Think about what you *really* want in your life. The idea of a favorite future should be with you for your entire life, a never-ending conversation with yourself. Be specific about your goals. If you say that you want to spend more time with your family, what does that really mean? What do you want to do with your children, grandchildren, siblings, or parents? What do you want to teach them, show them, experience with them?

One of my goals with my two young grandnephews when they come to visit every summer is to devote time to a new experience for them. I have shared their lessons in sailing, horseback riding, tennis, and surfing. It's quality time together, and they get exposed to things they might be inspired to pursue in their own favorite future. When any kid in our family turns sixteen years old, I offer them an experience at Outward Bound, one of the best organizations for experience-based outdoor learning and leadership for both youth and adults. I'm also planning a future trip to take a group of Clinton kids to Ireland to meet our extended family in County Monaghan, where my paternal grandfather emigrated from when he came to America in the 1920s. I'll be able to give them a tour of the house where their great-great-great-grandparents lived. They and their parents and a few of my siblings will spend time getting to know where we came from and how our Irish family thinks about their favorite future.

Another relationship that sometimes needs to be rethought is a long-term marriage. Do you have that nagging feeling that you and your partner have grown in divergent ways? Do you plan to do anything about it? More importantly, are you still in love with your partner? Were you ever really in love, or was it just convenient to marry the person you are with? It's tough to face this basic truth in our life, but we need to do it, to either find peace with it or move on.

Emily[13] was in her late forties when she made the tough decision to leave a marriage that wasn't working anymore. It was a brutal time for her, as she reflected that her husband, a lawyer, had manipulated it in such a way that she was left penniless—literally. With two kids (she shared custody with her husband), she had to find it in herself to move forward.

Emily had a small interior design business that allowed her to keep working, but it was tough. She took a small apartment and kept her attention on her own vision for herself, her kids, and her business. It took a few years, but she got her rhythm. Today her business is thriving; she bought her own house; and she has a new man in her life who adores her and vice versa.

Making the decision to find your new future doesn't happen in an instant. Of the people I interviewed for this book, each said it took them a year or two to formulate the plan that was right for them. Whether it was work, their personal life, or their lifestyle, they went deep inside themselves to truly understand what they wanted from their lives.

Julia[14] is in that process. An attorney by training, she works as the executive director of tax and payroll of a major university. But she is already thinking ahead. She is taking classes through the Wine & Spirits Education Trust, a London-based wine-education provider, resulting in a diploma that then leads to the master of wine studies qualification. She is also taking a set of classes through Washington State University's extension program to understand viticulture and enology, or wine making.

ROAR TIP

Take out a blank sheet of paper and write your own future, or start making notes on your laptop or phone as you go through your day. If you are becoming an empty nester in three years, it is not too early to start thinking about what's next. If your company is offering exit packages for early retirement and you are fifty-five years old, what do the numbers look like, and are you ready to step out into the unknown? Is now the time to chase your personal passion, purpose, or hobby by making it your life's work? If so, then it's time to ROAR!

She and her husband plan to move to the Porto region of northern Portugal and after a year or two there decide if they will start their own vineyard. It's still a few years away, but she is definitely constructing her favorite future now!

Only you can start writing that script, and only you can cast yourself as the lead in that production. If you adopt the right attitude, it can be exhilarating, taking you to places that will satisfy you for years. But remember, thinking about your favorite future is a lifelong pursuit, not just a one-time effort. You'll need to do it multiple times in your life between now and the end.

I'm fond of asking eighty-year-olds, *What is your favorite future?* Their answers always intrigue me. One gentleman has said that he is rewriting his resume because he thinks he would excel at selling luxury items like private airplanes. Another person said they want to live in France or Italy for a year, and others have said they want to teach what they know. I'm on the constant search for role models who are doing extraordinary things in their seventies and eighties, ignoring self-imposed ageism or the refrain that "you are too old to do that!"

In her book *Racing Age*, photojournalist Angela Jimenez has documented competitive masters track and field meets around the world. Seeing senior athletes participate in a five-thousand-meter run or throw a javelin is an inspiration as to what we can do at any time in our life.

ROAR TIP

Here is a simple exercise: You are ninety years old. Reflect back on your life. What did you accomplish? What was your legacy? Did you live the life that you wanted to live? That should be your active thinking, starting now, with an annual favorite-future check-in on what happened in the past year and what will happen in the next. What will be your story when it is told someday, when you are gone?

Regardless of your dream, it should never end. When my brother Joe said to me, "When are you going to stop?" my response was, "When I die."

ROAR: Chapter Takeaways

- Banish the word *retire*. My motto is to rewire and refire! What is your call to action?
- If that little voice in your head keeps telling you that you need a shift in life, listen to it! It will get louder and louder until you are forced to pay attention.
- Take yourself out of a bad situation and write your own narrative. Want to quit a job? Make your plan and build your next step. Only you have the power to "rewrite" your future!
- Confused about what to do next? What did you want to be when you were ten, twelve, fifteen years old? Your inner child is still there, seeking your attention; take time each day to reconnect, whether through meditation or quiet time.
- Don't avoid the roadblocks or let setbacks stop you from pursuing your dreams—the only way out is to go in deep!
- Start to plan your future two to three years before you embark on it. Write it down. Study it. Is it the track you want to take? You might live to be ninety, so this should be something you do for the rest of your life. Make a change at sixty and be empowered to make one at seventy or eighty!
- Envision the future self you want to be. Vision-board it; write the future story of your life. What do you want later generations to know about you? How do you want to be remembered?

PART II

Own Who
You Are

3

Own Where You Came From

Where you will sit when you are old shows
where you stood in youth.
—Yoruba proverb

We all have a past. We all have baggage. We all have moments of *woulda, coulda,* and *shoulda.* We are all coming from that past to face our future. You are a composite of those experiences, and there's not much you can do about them now. You have to own them as what makes you special and unique. In this chapter, you'll read stories of people who learned to own where they came from to break through to their next life chapter.

We all have moments of woulda, coulda, *and* shoulda. *We are all coming from that past to face our future.*

When we hit our forties, we begin to see what has been working in our lives and what hasn't. Our past begins to catch up with us, if we have floundered in work or in a relationship. In the ROAR Into survey, 43 percent of the respondents said that they tend to dwell on their mistakes and rehash them. It's a lot of wasted energy; what's done is done. Don't obsess over the past!

We think about our parents and our upbringing, and we sometimes slip into laying blame in places that may be misguided. I had an uncle who spent his whole life blaming my grandparents for his lack of direction and focus. Even at an early age, I wondered why he didn't take responsibility for his own life and stop blaming them.

In midlife, we start to gain clarity and begin to realize that if we don't course-correct, we'll just stay stuck.

> **ROAR TIP**
>
> *How do you have your own awakening?* Start by embracing where you came from and getting over your embarrassments, regrets, or sources of unhappiness. Choose to awaken into your future. And forgive yourself for any past mistakes; dwelling on them is a waste of energy.

When I think back on my early life, I realize that I had few prospects for a better future, although I didn't quite know it then. We were a poor, working-class family. My father was a telephone lineman, and my mother stayed home to raise six children. We had started out in the public-housing projects of St. Clair Village in Pittsburgh's South Hills, ultimately moving to a small three-story house in the Carrick section of the city. The first floor had three rooms: a kitchen, a family room, and my parents' bedroom. The three rooms on the second floor were rented to outsiders, who shared the same entrance to the house. The third-floor attic was a makeshift bedroom, where my three sisters slept on one side and my two brothers and I slept on the other side.

Since the second-floor bathroom was for the renters, our family shared a bathroom in the basement. My father built a cinder-block room around a freestanding toilet and shower stall that we all used. The laundry tubs served as a place to brush our teeth and wash our hands. Needless to say, the conditions weren't ideal. When I looked around me, most of our neighbors didn't have it much better. In my city high school, most of the kids were children of steel-mill workers or other laborer jobs, with everyone struggling to make ends meet.

Fortunately, for our family, there was always food and clothing and heat in the winter, along with great love from our parents, who did their best with what we had. Years later, I learned that my mother would forgo makeup for weeks so that she could spend the money on food, while my father worked long overtime hours to make sure that extra money would come in for our needs. We would take Sunday rides for entertainment, oftentimes to the local airport to watch the planes take off and land, have picnics in a city park, or at times, rush to watch baseball at Forbes Field during the sixth inning, since you could enter the ballpark without paying once the game was that far along. Our lives were simple, but we always felt like a family that was together.

As the oldest of six, I often experienced the load of babysitting, along with a constant list of chores, from mowing the lawn to shoveling snow to doing dishes. My sister Kate, two years younger, was my main helpmate, as the four others were still too young. It taught me at an early age about responsibility and delegating, especially as the other kids grew older. By the time I scored the neighborhood paper route, hand-delivering nearly a hundred subscriptions of the *Pittsburgh Press*, I was able to off-load some of my chores to the younger kids. That job also taught me about the importance of collecting money, saving money, and thinking about money as a means to an end. At twelve, it was my first experience in business!

There weren't a lot of role models around, even in my own family. With the exception of one relative who had gone to night school to study accounting, no one had ever gone to college. My maternal grandmother, one of ten children, never finished high school, nor did several of her siblings, two of whom became homeless. My maternal grandfather went to a trade school to be an undertaker, like his mother, who had started a funeral home to cater to the Lithuanian community. To make ends meet, he also worked as a night-shift laborer at the Jones and Laughlin steel mill. On my father's side, my grandparents were both immigrants from Ireland, with no real education.

All in all, it was pretty bleak on the education front, something that I had begun to realize was the key to a better life. Although only high school graduates themselves, my parents were wonderful about exposing us to culture. We went to local museums and art fairs. Every Friday night, we had a family outing to the library (where we could take a maximum of five books for the week), sometimes stopping for ice cream on the way home. I can still remember the smell of the books stacked on the shelves and the process of checking them out, as the aide stamped the card at the front of the book indicating when it was due.

When we got home, I would immediately start reading, sometimes finishing all of my books by the end of the weekend. From the Hardy Boys fiction series to history and geography and biographies, through words I saw that there was a bigger world out there. In high school, one of my English teachers saw my innate hunger for books to read and would give me extra novels that I would devour late into the night. To this day, reading a book every two weeks is one of my passions, whether it is a novel, a biography, or a book on current events. Reading is an intoxication for the mind and the soul. As my friend Colette said about her father, who was unable to get a formal education, "He traveled on the wings of philosophers, poets, and writers."

Once upon a time, I was embarrassed about my humble beginnings, never discussing them with anyone. But at a certain point in my adulthood, when I started achieving success, where I came from became a badge of honor. The journey began when I traveled crosstown to the University of Pittsburgh to study economics and political science. I knew that if I didn't find a way to fund my own education, it wouldn't happen, so I juggled multiple jobs and took out student loans. My parents had five other kids to worry about. Ultimately, I came to learn that owning my beginnings was not only liberating, it also pushed me forward. After all, if I could find my way to a better life from where I started, anyone could. It wasn't until I was in college that I actually began to believe that it could happen!

In my mid-twenties, I continued my education journey by taking classes at night to earn my MBA while I was building my publishing career. Three of my siblings went on to college, one to nursing school, and one sister launched her own successful fitness business. In the next generation, we already have a kid with a PhD, one with a master's, two who have undergraduate degrees, and more graduates to come. Education has now become a part of our family's value system.

My own parents found a new path for their lives, too. In his late twenties, my father got involved in union politics, first with the Federation of Telephone Workers of Pennsylvania and then with the Communication Workers of America. He was elected president of his local union, and then became full-time regional vice president of the union in his forties. From there, he became the union's executive vice president of the state of Pennsylvania and then president, before retiring at sixty-seven. His pivot into full-time union work gave him a purpose that he thrived on and is how he met his current wife, Kathleen, who was also a union executive.

After being a stay-at-home mom for years, my mother found her way to a midlife career too. At first, she worked as a hostess in a restaurant and then as an administrative assistant at the University of Pittsburgh so that several of my siblings could get a college degree through her tuition benefits. But it wasn't until she was in her late forties that she found a job she was passionate about for nearly twenty-five years.

When my brother Matthew and I sent our parents on a first-time trip to Europe for their anniversary, it sparked something in her that would change her life forever. The experience of that two-week trip led to an idea to become a travel agent, a job that she charmed her way into with no experience. She started from the ground up, learning the reservation systems and all the details involved in the business of being an agent at a local travel agency. Not only did it give her joy and excitement to plan trips for people, it also afforded her the ability to see the world—she ultimately visited nearly forty countries. At fifty-seven, she backpacked through Europe for several months, taking in museums and art galleries and local history. Her reimagined life took her to places far beyond her own dreams and expectations, giving her an education that had eluded her as a young woman.

Did I forget to mention that in her early life, my mother had actually been a nun and then was in the US Air Force? Obviously she went through a lot of reimagining from an early age. When she was sixty-four years old, she asked my father for a divorce after forty years. It was not an earth-shattering event; it was simply that she had a vision for the rest of her life that was too far from what my father wanted to do. For the next twenty-four years, she traveled and read and even moved to England for a short stint. Most women in her neighborhood were in awe that she could step out and live a completely different life for herself.

When she left us a month before her eighty-ninth birthday, dozing off and not waking up, she had in fact acted on her last reimagined self, as she had hoped that she might leave this earth in exactly the way that she left. When I would ask my mother what her favorite future was, she would answer, "To have a peaceful death." And she did.

Even though my parents didn't have a lot of money around, both my mother and father found a way to have experiences that brought personal fulfillment and enriched their lives, which inspired all of us along the way. Once, when I was being interviewed for a podcast, the host asked me if I was such a high achiever to make up for my humble beginnings. My response was quick: "Sure. The bucket was completely empty, and I had to fill it up!" My parents did the same, even though they were in their late forties before they could start on their own journeys.

My story is not a unique one. Plenty of well-known people came from humble beginnings, many worse than mine. Oprah Winfrey has been very forthcoming about her struggles, as has J. D. Vance, author of *Hillbilly Elegy*, who embraced his Appalachian background to educate people who look down on "hillbillies" but don't fully understand the challenges they face. Many of us watched *The Pursuit of Happyness*, a movie starring Will Smith as Chris Gardner. This biographical drama is about a man who found his way from homelessness to becoming a multimillionaire through his talents in selling stocks, leading to his own company, Gardner Rich.

My longtime colleague David Carey[1] is another example of someone who owned and remembered where he came from. The son of a grocery-store cashier and homemaker in Long Beach, California, David went on to exceptional success in the magazine industry. Although he had experienced some pretty heady things, including visiting the White House and attending the Grammys, he was always conscious of separating his professional identity from his personal identity. Along the way, he looked for role models and, in fact, was a role model himself. "When you grow up in a lower-income household and you achieve success, you ultimately find yourself with a great deal of gratitude," he said.

Surrounded by the trappings of a fast-paced and glamourous New York life, he cultivated his own path, determining what was right for him and his family. Happy to hop the subway or take a taxi instead of a hired car service in getting around town, he focused on achievement rather than the external trappings of success. He and his wife, Lauri, raised two sets of twins, who all carry a strong work ethic and positive approach to life.

David led a disciplined life, saving his money for the day when he would be able to step out of his high-powered job, a decision he made at fifty-seven. At first, he was going to do a year of "intellectual tourism," as he called it, stringing together a list of places to attend, from the Aspen Ideas Festival to programs at Stanford or other universities that would give him some new things to think about.

Along the way, David discovered the Advanced Leadership Initiative at Harvard University and applied for admittance. The program, comprising fifteen fellow partners, is a full calendar year of lectures and projects that help executives and leaders get ready for their next chapter as well as teaching them how to apply their specific talents to have an impact on major social problems, from environmental to health and welfare issues. Once he was accepted, he and Lauri moved to Boston for the year. As a spouse, she was also able to take classes on the Harvard campus. "Ultimately, I wanted to give away all of my suits and find a new path that would be meaningful to me," David said.

At first, he thought he might take on a leadership role at a nonprofit, but after the Harvard program, he returned to a corporate position at his company, focusing on corporate social responsibility and other key initiatives. And the good news? He doesn't need to wear a suit.

You don't have to go to Harvard to experience an advanced leadership program, as they are offered by many schools, among them the University of Nevada, Reno, and Vanderbilt University in Nashville. There are also programs at state universities, such as the University of Minnesota's Advanced Career Initiative, which is an affordable yearlong program designed to help adults fifty-five and over launch their next career. Unlike many programs designed for top-level executives, this one is for anyone who wants to find their next level of growth.

One of my favorite stories is about Jim O'Callaghan, who lives in Dublin, Ireland. He was managing a newsagent shop in Dublin when, in his late fifties, he enrolled in night school to get the college degree he never had. He juggled work and school, graduating in his early sixties. But he then went on to study drawing and visual investigation at the National College of Art and Design when he heard about a job at the bookstore at the National Gallery of Ireland. He applied and got the job, ultimately progressing to giving tours and lectures until he retired at sixty-nine years old in 2010.

Then, it was on to his next move, which was to become one of Dublin's well-known street photographers, as he roamed the city to chronicle everyday life in the Irish capital. (Did I mention that Jim was inspired by Irish artist Flora Mitchell, about whom, incidentally, he wrote his thesis for a master of letters degree from University College Dublin?) As he approaches eighty, Jim continues to take photographs with the goal of turning his work into a book. Something tells me there is a whole new chapter ahead of him.[2]

ROAR TIP

Your personal ambition and passion should be what drives you. What have you put on a back burner that is getting a lot hotter?

On the flip side, some people were born into highly successful and wealthy families. I've met many of them in my New York life. They have a different burden in that some of them never find their way, almost paralyzed with their good fortune. Yet many go on to professional and personal success, giving back to their communities in ways that are cru- cial for a healthy society. And there are people who went to Ivy League schools but have not had significant success in the world, while others who went to state schools or even dropped out of college went on to huge career success.

In his book *Where You Go Is Not Who You'll Be*, Frank Bruni lays out the case that it is your own personal drive and ambition that propel you through life. That sentiment is not only relevant for where you go to college, it also has meaning for your entire life. To limit yourself by your education, your experience, where you live, or your family situation is creating your own jail cell. It becomes your crutch, your excuse as to why you can't move in a new direction.

There are too many self-imposed restrictions in our lives—based on where we have come from or what we have experienced to date—that keep us from growing. Those restrictions are also where we come from in our twenties and thirties. Let's say that you squandered away those years in a directionless manner or jumping from job to job or staying in a bad relationship. There's not much you can do about that now, except to own it and move on.

> **ROAR TIP**
>
> Take an inventory of the good, the bad, and the ugly from a broken relationship, and boil it down to its essence. Being brutally honest with yourself is always the challenge, because you are also at fault when a relationship ends. Understand it. Own it. And carry on. If you are struggling with it, talk to friends, join a support group, talk to your spiritual leader. You owe it to yourself to come to peace with it.

There is nothing worse than that forty-five-year-old who is still complaining about being done wrong by their college sweetheart! That person might have been heartbroken, but what has their life been since then? Think about it. If you haven't had another meaningful relationship, are you in your own way? A friend had someone break up with him when he was in his early fifties. He had always been the one who would break off a relationship, so it was a new concept for him. I said, "Welcome to the human race." Everyone has had their heart broken or had an unrequited love. The pain is real, but you can't wallow in it. That relationship is over, gone, done. Start your clean slate.

Rebecca,[3] in her mid-fifties, bemoaned the fact that she has never been able to maintain a long-term relationship. She was a bit shocked when I suggested to her that maybe she really wasn't interested in a relationship, so why did she keep obsessing about it? Did I mention that she had broken off several engagements? In her relationship attempts, she was preoccupied with her definition of a perfect mate. At her age, she still hadn't come to terms with the fact that there is no such thing. Relationships are up and down and can be messy and annoying. It goes with the territory. For whatever reason, she had been unable to learn this or accept it. Hopefully, she will find her path, as it is never too late to find someone to love and be loved by.

We all know people who suddenly realize in their early forties that they haven't accomplished much in the way of work or professional development. Some get stuck in life, frustrated that they cannot seem to progress. If you are at that point, now is the time to step back and figure out what you truly want. It's never too late.

> ### ROAR TIP
>
> Sometimes you just have to jump in, knowing that you are vulnerable and open to potential hurt. But by jumping, at least you will lead a richer life, one filled with emotions and memories—reminders that you have lived! As Andy Dufresne said in the movie *The Shawshank Redemption*, "Get busy living or get busy dying!"[4]

My brother Joe, for instance, graduated with a degree in psychology, with the goal of becoming a counselor for youth programs. He is one of the smartest, most knowledgeable, and funniest people I know. Yet he got sidetracked for years, working in dead-end jobs. When he was in his late fifties, I suggested that he pick up his dream and go back to the goal he had in his twenties. It might take some work, some volunteering, another degree or certificate, but it could mean a twenty-year run in a job that would give him satisfaction and growth. (I'm still working on that idea with him, but he knows it is his decision to move it forward. As his big brother, I will always give him my support to make it happen.)

For someone who has been on a career track and feels stalled, the question is *What is the plan?* Leave your industry? Retool? Rethink your goals? A mid-career executive may not think they have the background to advance to the next level, but oftentimes that is their own roadblock. If advancing is the ambition, what is stopping you from figuring out the path you need to take to get there? If you don't see it happening in the company you are in, change companies. Your experience up to this point is all you have to show for some twenty years of work. Now is the moment to assess what you like to do and what you don't like to do. If you have been in line sales and want to be a manager, what is stopping you from doing that? If you realize that you hate being a manager, what is your plan to return to the sales team or find another path?

Cate Murden[5] led the fast-paced executive life in London's bustling advertising and media agency business. As she approached her forties, she had the double whammy of major stress and being a victim of downsizing. What did she do, you ask? She did what she calls a very good self-audit and decided to commit herself to helping people in the creative, media, and tech industries deal with stress and a whole lot more. Now in her mid-forties, she has a thriving business called PUSH with seven core team members, over a hundred life and well-being coaches, and a roster of clients that would be the envy of any business.

PUSH has a terrific tagline: "We help companies be more human." The mission is to ensure that no one ever feels like they are just existing or dreading work. One of the goals is to help people achieve peak performance by unlocking their full human potential. In my conversation with Cate, her passion came through as she described how one of the programs—one-to-one coaching and psychotherapy for professionals in the area of mental health—gave people the tools and framework to learn new ways to manage their minds, reframe a situation, and get results.

One of my favorite PUSH mantras is to find work–life brilliance, not work–life balance. Cate has big plans for the company: new app technologies in the works, more investment capital to expand (she started the company with money from her exit package and got two friends to invest in the original start-up phase). She sees PUSH providing more insights on how work will change during and after the COVID-19 pandemic. From her own challenging life moment, Cate did an about-face and dove into the industry she knew—but from a completely different angle. She gets to work with creative and interesting people, as she did in the past, but now her focus is on how to help them understand that being human is their superpower as they find their true strengths.

Sometimes a life experience can awaken you to a place you know you need to go. Kristine Welker[6] was a successful businesswoman with a husband and three kids. She described herself as driven and fearless, and she made a conscious decision to keep working hard when her kids were young, thinking about her goal of financial security that would be at the end of an intense twenty-to-thirty-year career.

When her son was eight years old, he was diagnosed with muscular dystrophy, a disease that causes progressive weakness and loss of muscle mass. The family snapped into action to get him the care he needed, but Kristine admitted she was still so caught up in work that she would sometimes forget to set up her son's medical appointments. That is, until she awakened to the knowledge that her son's health—not another business trip—should be her top priority. For starters, she joined the board of the Muscular Dystrophy Association to learn as much as she could about the condition.

"It made me rethink everything. I was about to turn fifty, and I went into a year of reviewing my whole life. I knew that I couldn't control my son's progress with his diagnosis, but I might be able to control other things by helping out the organization," she said.

At that time, Kristine stepped out of her high-powered, successful job to devote herself full-time to her son's health. People were stunned, and her kids were fearful about her decision, but she knew that while she had had great business success, she now wanted to take those learnings and apply them to her new interest. She also wrote a personal thesis to live her life with more purpose, telling her children that it is not just about net worth but also about self-worth. "It also felt good to tear off some past labels. I realized that I wasn't as fearless as I thought, but actually a bit fearful. I had to own that and ultimately it was okay. It became my motivating force," she said.

Applying her business skills to the organization, Kristine brought new thinking and innovation to its mission. Her contribution was so impactful that the board asked her to step in as interim CEO when a decision was made for a change in leadership. During that year, she worked on a strategic plan to move the organization forward. Passing the baton to the new CEO, she continued on the board and the executive committee, and then agreed to become chief of staff for the organization. She continues to be passionate about its work. Her son is now sixteen and doing well, and his mother knows more about his condition than many doctors!

When I asked her how it felt during that change process, she said that her best advice to people is to think of it as a "you-turn." "We don't give ourselves permission to make a change," she explained. "My past achievements were great, but I took all that I knew and leveraged them into this new focus."

Not everyone has to make the decision to step out like Kristine did, but she made the assessment of where she had come from at that point in her life and decided what she needed to do next.

I had my own experience with this in my fifties, when someone was brought into the company above me, in a job I had hoped would be mine. Although I had gotten a promotion in the reorganization, I wasn't so sure I would stick it out. After some soul-searching and some long runs in the park, I decided to give it a year, which turned into nine years working with my Hearst colleague David Carey, mentioned earlier in this chapter, who had come into the role. He and I clicked, and he treated me as his partner from the start. We and the other members of the executive team outperformed our industry peers, with better results than theirs and our successors' to this day. He and I were named the media executive team of the year by one of our leading trade magazines. For me, it was the right decision then and in hindsight. During those years, I had many calls to become the CEO of this company or that company, but I never felt I would have had the kind of rich professional experience I had by staying at Hearst.

As I've traveled the world, it has become more and more apparent to me that so many of us have an incredible gift: the gift of being able to find ways to better our lives through education, hard work, and commitment to our goals. There are still countless disadvantaged people who struggle to find a course—and many inequities that prevent it—but they still have the best shot of moving their lives forward through perseverance and a commitment to a better future.

Deb Haaland exemplifies perseverance and commitment. A member of the Laguna Pueblo people, she identifies as a thirty-fifth-generation New Mexican. Haaland didn't start college until she was twenty-eight years old, and she gave birth to a daughter four days after graduating. As a single mother, she started a salsa company but had to rely on food stamps and at times the kindness of friends to provide shelter for her and her daughter. Yet she pushed onward and earned a law degree at the University of New Mexico. Haaland became the first of two Native American women elected to the US Congress in 2018. She then made history by being selected as the Secretary of the Interior in the Biden administration, the first Native American to serve in a cabinet position. Her story is what I call an American "wow." Hard work, drive, and a commitment to find a path forward for herself—she is an inspiration to all of us. Did I mention that she was sixty years old when Biden picked her for her role? Haaland is just getting started![7]

Too often, people don't own their good fortune or realize that what they have is unique. In America, I've always been impressed by the incredible work ethic and drive that so many young immigrants and their families have. I am similarly impressed by the legions of disadvantaged American-born people who can see a future with endless possibilities, driven only by what they imagine that they can accomplish.

We all need to own that where we come from is an enormous benefit, allowing us to become our true selves.

All around the world, companies, organizations, and individuals are doing a lot of positive work to help people find better ways to build their lives through educational opportunities and advancements in the workplace. We need to have systems in place that help those who want to build a better future, first for themselves and then for their families. We all need to own that where we come from is an enormous benefit, allowing us to become our true selves. We all have the opportunity to find our own personal path.

But none of us can do it unless we own our past, forgive ourselves for our mistakes, and begin anew. We don't know what is ahead, but we know today.

ROAR TIP

Whether it is your beginnings or your midlife or your post-career life, owning where you have come from is the start. From there, you can dream, plan, and set your course for the newly reimagined you. It's all possible.

I once read a quote from the Zimbabwean-born Canadian writer Matshona Dhliwayo: "Yesterday says, 'Forget me, but learn from me.' Today says, 'Embrace me, yet utilize me.' Tomorrow says, 'Anticipate me, then prepare for me.'"[8]

ROAR: Chapter Takeaways

- Like me, you can come from a place with little to nothing except your drive, your dreams, your ambition, and an education. Own your past and become the master of your own destiny.
- We all have regrets; don't let them linger. Practice self-forgiveness. Learn from the experience, then release yourself from what was and focus on where you will go next!
- The impact you can have on your family, friends, and community is endless. What can you do to help set someone on their own new future journey? Is there an opportunity to become a mentor? One of the perks of having lived a full life is the wisdom and experience you have to share. Check out AARP's volunteer-based tutoring program, Experience Corps, as a way to contribute.
- Give yourself permission to change, whatever age you are. And remember, you get to decide what that looks like for you, whether it's a change in career, a change in where you live, or simply learning a new hobby—no change is insignificant if it inspires you to ROAR.
- Never give up on love. It's the fuel that will bring you the moments you will truly cherish. Step out and look for it. As humans, we all deserve love.

4

Own Your Numbers

The truth is, when a number—your age—becomes your identity,
you've given away your power to choose your future.
—Richard J. Leider and Alan M. Webber, *Life Reimagined*

This chapter will teach you how to own your numbers to move forward.
Let's start with the key numbers for personal physical health, which is
the foundation of everything and should be your number one priority. That
is followed by healthy financial numbers, an embracing of your age, actual
numbers against your life goals, and the "ultimate number." Yes, we are all
going to die someday. Have you done any of the work to be prepared?

*Personal physical health, which is the foundation of everything . . .
should be your number one priority.*

I'm always surprised when I ask someone around fifty years old what
their blood pressure is, and they have no idea! By the time you reach
fifty, you should have a strong handle on all of your health numbers.
You should also know the importance of a particular age with regard
to certain tests, such as your first colonoscopy at forty-five. (A family
member who didn't have his first one until seventy learned that he had
colon cancer, which led to his premature death a few years later.)

This is pretty straightforward advice: Get smart about your
health, especially as you age. For more specific information, I turned

to Dr. Keith LaScalea,[1] an internist and associate professor at Weill Cornell Medicine, an academic medical center in New York City. Dr. LaScalea, who is forty-eight, practices what he preaches by keeping tabs on his health, eating right, and staying fit. In 2020, he finished running fifty marathons, one in each of the fifty states, the final run being in Maui, Hawaii. His total marathon count is sixty-five!

According to Dr. LaScalea, your blood pressure is one of the most important numbers—for everyone—because it is the one that can lead to heart attacks, strokes, and premature death. Whether it is controlled by lifestyle or by medication, know this number. He could not emphasize it enough. In fact, he suggests buying a blood-pressure arm cuff at your local pharmacy, so you can monitor your own blood pressure on a regular basis. His advice for the number is that people age forty-five and up should be somewhere around 120/80 or below. He did add that as people age to sixty-five and up, that number may become a bit more liberal in range to minimize hypotension (low blood pressure) and falls. His range for an ideal resting heart rate for someone forty-five and up is between fifty and eighty beats per minute, a number usually based on lifestyle.[2]

Part of overall health also includes knowing your BMI (body mass index, a weight-to-height ratio), noting that you want to be below twenty-five. (Go to cdc.gov for an easy calculator.) A BMI between twenty-five and thirty means you are overweight, over thirty is obese, and above forty is morbidly obese. We all know too many people over fifty years old who let their weight get out of control, and that is not healthy, particularly since it takes a lot longer to take weight off as we age.

ROAR TIP

Ideally, you should maintain your body weight over time. My own monitor is the "five-pound rule." If I notice that my weight has been creeping up, above my ideal of 175 pounds, I cut out desserts or that extra glass of wine, or I run an extra few miles. Managing those choices is a lot easier to handle than suddenly realizing you have gained twenty pounds!

Dr. LaScalea likes to watch other numbers among aging patients, starting with the fasting blood sugar level (hopefully under a hundred), because diabetes can develop as we age. Cholesterol numbers should be monitored, keeping LDL (which is the bad kind that collects in the walls of your blood vessels) below one hundred (depending on risk factors) and HDL (which is the good cholesterol) above forty. He also recommends a thyroid test every five years, along with monitoring liver and kidney numbers.

For men, the PSA (prostate-specific antigen) test is critical, with a goal below the number two. This test screens for prostate cancer, and screening should entail a conversation between you and your doctor. For women, it's important to monitor bone density (especially ten years after menopause); it can be assessed through a DEXA scan that can diagnose osteoporosis.

When I asked Dr. LaScalea if there was anything else that the average sixty-year-old should focus on, he admitted that one size doesn't fit all, but he did have some other suggestions that are worth reporting. People should have a regular relationship with a doctor—someone who knows you and monitors your health progress through life. A physician who knows you over time can more easily detect when something more serious is occurring with you, often picking things up earlier than a walk-in clinic is likely to do.

It's also important to watch any health issues that you might already have, or to track your family history and how it might impact you. Identifying issues early on gives you the opportunity to manage them into a healthier life. As a two-time skin cancer survivor, I'm diligent about visiting my dermatologist on a regular basis to look me over head to toe for anything suspicious.

Dr. LaScalea believes in what many people know about maintaining good health, but you also need to put these important lifestyle approaches in to practice: you need to eat right, have a fitness regimen, and sleep right.

As for diet, Dr. LaScalea advocates a plant-based diet rich in fruits, vegetables, seeds, and nuts, with the goal of reducing the amount of processed foods we consume. He recommends a Mediterranean diet, since studies have shown that longevity is correlated with this eating pattern. According to him, reducing the amount of meat in our diet is important as we age, since most large nutritional studies have shown that populations who eat small amounts of meat have the lowest incidences of heart attacks, strokes, and early death. I also asked him, "What is the one bit of food advice that you would give everyone?" His answer was to eat a salad every day. It fills you up with valuable vitamins and fiber, and it displaces the need for other kinds of food that may be less healthy.

Since he is an avid marathoner, Dr. LaScalea also emphasizes the importance of exercise in one's daily life. "Everyone needs to do some type of exercise every week, period," he said. His advice is to find an exercise that you enjoy, something that is convenient, and partner up with someone to make it fun. Most people can walk, and that may lead to running, and that may lead to a 10k or more. And that can happen at any age.

I've always been inspired by Fauja Singh, who couldn't walk until he was five years old. As a young adult, he was able to begin running, but soon the demands of life took over. After several personal tragedies, he began running again, and at eighty-nine years old (yes, eighty-nine!) he became a serious runner. At ninety-three, Fauja completed a marathon in six hours and fifty-four minutes, and at the grand age of one hundred, he set eight world age-group records in one day. When I ran the Toronto Marathon in 2011, I watched him become the first one-hundred-year-old to finish a marathon—in eight hours, eleven minutes, and six seconds![3]

So, if you are sixty years old and think you can't start running, get a checkup from your doctor, buy a pair of running shoes, and get out to your local track. Fauja went roaring into a fitness regimen that is the envy of everyone! If walking or running is not your thing, then try something else. Hire a personal trainer, experiment with weights and exercises, walk steps, try kayaking, tai chi, yoga, swimming, bicycling. If you are an avid golfer, keep at it. Find something.

There are four key things to remember if you are starting a fitness regimen from scratch. Dr. LaScalea encourages his patients to consider cardiovascular exercise, weight training, flexibility, and balance as the four domains of a complete exercise regimen. The last two are especially important as we age. It's as simple as Googling "balance exercises" to create a morning regimen to keep you strong and steady.

> **ROAR TIP**
>
> For anyone over forty-five, your health formula should be simple: know your health numbers, find your nutritional path, get good sleep, and exercise regularly.

Aside from my own running regimen, I do a gym workout twice a week, I hike whenever I can, and I mix things up with occasional cycling or kayaking. Skiing is my favorite sport, and I'm still at it. Once, when I was coming back from a day of skiing, an older man stepped onto the van that was taking us all to the parking lot. He was fit and tan and had a sparkle in his eye.

"How was your day?" I asked him. "You must have a long history of skiing; I'll bet you are pretty good."

"Well," he said, "I tried skiing for the first time when I was sixty-five, and now I'm eighty-five and I love every minute of it."

"You are definitely my inspiration," I said. "I want to be you at eighty-five!"

> **ROAR TIP**
>
> Loads of books have been written about nutrition and eating right, as well as about maintaining some type of fitness regimen, particularly as we age. Plus, there are podcasts, lectures, fitness trainers, videos on YouTube, and experts at your local college who can help find the right advice for you. One of my favorite books of all time is the huge bestseller *Younger Next Year: Live Strong, Fit, Sexy, and Smart—Until You're 80 and Beyond*, written by Chris Crowley and Henry S. Lodge, MD, with Allan J. Hamilton, MD. It is a compendium of tips and ideas that help us age in a dynamic way.

One last item to add to the list for a healthy life: the importance of sleep. According to the National Sleep Foundation, people over age sixty-five should get at least seven to eight hours of sleep every night to stay both physically and mentally well as we age. It helps your mood, lets your body restore itself from stress, helps you maintain your weight, and lets your brain clear itself of harmful toxins. The benefit of a good night's sleep is becoming more and more apparent for healthy aging. Arianna Huffington, cofounder of the *Huffington Post* and author of fifteen books, has become a global advocate of the importance of sleep. Her book *The Sleep Revolution: Transforming Your Life, One Night at a Time* is a must-read. As for me, I'm a good sleeper because I stay active every day. And when it's time for bed, I make a point to put my phone away at least an hour beforehand. I keep the room cool and dark and think about my best accomplishment of the day. It's a positive way to close out the day and ensure a peaceful night's sleep.

In the ROAR Into survey, 41 percent of respondents said they are very concerned about money for their future, while nearly 50 percent said they either didn't factor in all the real costs of their post-working life or really weren't sure if they had. More than half (52 percent) of respondents ages forty-five to fifty-nine and 41 percent of respondents sixty to seventy-five reported that they currently do not have enough money saved to retire.

ROAR TIP

Know your financial numbers. One of my favorite books about this topic is *The Number: What Do You Need for the Rest of Your Life, and What Will It Cost?* by Lee Eisenberg. The "number" he alludes to in the title is the amount of money you need so you can step out of your main career. That's something we all need to be thinking about, especially in a world with fewer pensions, the uncertainty of Social Security in the future, and low interest rates on our savings.

If you don't have a financial advisor or family member who is savvy about this topic, there are plenty of free or low-cost tools online to start working up your calculations. To gain some insights on the topic, I spoke to Martin Gruber,[4] a senior financial advisor at a large multinational firm that works with individuals and families. He shared with me some of his best advice.

According to Martin, the number one priority is to determine how much your lifestyle costs now, and how much it will cost in the future to maintain the lifestyle that you want. Let's say you are contemplating retirement from your main source of income and you have determined that you need to generate $100,000 after tax for your annual expenses without tapping into your principal. Assuming no other income sources, you will need $160,000 of pretax income (based on a 38 percent tax rate). In order to realize the $100,000 per year, you will need more than $2 million in income-generating assets (from brokerage or 401K investments) based on a 5% rate of return. You can subtract any pension payments or Social Security payments from the $160,000, keeping in mind that they are taxable items. Can you get to your number, the number that you have determined is right for you?

> **ROAR TIP**
>
> The median net income is $58,600 and the median net worth of all US families is $121,700, according to the Federal Reserve's "2019 Survey of Consumer Finances."[5] A family's average net worth varies across age, race, location, and education level. You can determine your own median net worth through various online calculators and tools that are free on the internet.

What's your number or goal number for when you get to that age range? Lots of decisions need to be made through this process. Should you sell your house and invest the proceeds, while taking on a rental? That approach gets you out of the never-ending costs of homeowning, from appliance breakdowns to property repairs. Should you move to one of the lower-cost housing states, such as Louisiana, Arizona, or New Mexico? Or move to one of the seven states that have no state income tax? That includes Florida, Texas, Montana, Wyoming, Washington,

Nevada, and Alaska. Many of these moves can help to preserve your annual income, stretching it further. You can also check out the World Health Organization's online global network of age-friendly cities and communities for ideas about your next lifestyle move.

My friend Andy Carter decided to leave the high cost of New York City and move to Bucks County, Pennsylvania, which was within driving distance of his family and friends. By moving, he cut his housing costs in half, as well as reducing other daily needs.

According to Martin, there are at least five key aspects that you need to consider while you are working on your number:

- Have a plan and a goal for ages fifty, sixty, seventy, and beyond.
- At this stage of life, you should be living within your means and managing "smart debt." If you are still in your forties, Martin's recommendation is to lock in debt for as long as you can and as cheaply as you can. A solid example of this is the thirty-year mortgage, especially if interest rates are low. Low-cost debt is good debt.
- Contribute to your 401(k) at the full maximum and company match (because that's free money). If you don't take advantage of this investment in your own future, you are missing out on a solid benefit. Add to your 401(k) through savings and investments for future cash flow. The compounding effect is also another form of "free money" to be used for your future.
- As you get closer to your retirement from your main job, live more within your means than you may have done in the past. In other words, don't go out and lease a luxury car with a high monthly payment when you are trying to put that extra cash to work for your future.
- Do the homework to see how you can preserve the capital that you do have: How do you plan to grow it, and how do you plan to spend it? If you are forty-five, what do you want your financial situation to be at fifty-five? At sixty? At sixty-five? What's your plan to get there? If you are sixty, what is your financial state of affairs right now, and are you ready for the next twenty years?

ROAR TIP

Many people don't want to do the hard, honest work of facing their money reality, but to successfully ROAR into a new life, you need to make sure you have the financial foundation to get there. The sooner you own your finances, the quicker you can make plans and take action to ensure a comfortable future.

Margaret and Bob Pardini[6] are like most middle-class Americans. She runs a small business out of their Pennsylvania home, and he is a master plumber. Their only son, a pharmacist, now lives across the country in California. In their late fifties, they have put together a five-year plan to ROAR out of the life that they have been living for decades: they are going to save as much money as possible, then sell their house, quit their jobs, and move to Ajijic, Mexico, a town on Lake Chapala, near Guadalajara, joining the thousands of other expats who have started a new life there.

ROAR TIP

Plenty of NGOs (nongovernmental organizations), religious organizations, foundations, and government organizations such as the Peace Corps would welcome you to become a part of their efforts around the world. Using whatever experience you've had is one way to find where and how you might be most helpful. Your skills and knowledge could help address any number of needs.

Once they knew that they wanted to leave the harsh winters of the Northeast, they took annual trips to various places in the US and in Mexico to see where they might settle. They fell in love with Ajijic because of its temperate climate, affordable cost of living, and established community. Now they go there every year to explore where they might live and what they might do as a new chapter, as they head into their early sixties. Moving to another part of your country or even to a different country can be a means of having an adventure, and there are lots of ways you can do it.

Countries such as Mexico, Costa Rica, Panama, and Portugal are only a few examples of welcoming places that allow you to stretch your dollar with housing, healthcare, and living costs. Start a Google search and soon you too will be dreaming about a second chapter in a place that inspires discovery. All it takes is imagination and a sense of adventure—and discipline. Like the Pardinis, you will need to home in on your finances and the end goal. In their case, they think that they can get there in five years to join many others who have gone before them.

ROAR TIP

Own your age–and be proud of it! Start saying it out loud to people!

Stop being vague by saying, "I have over thirty years' experience," when you've been working for forty-five years! Everyone can figure out how old you are anyway, so own that number. If you are internet dating or meeting a potential mate for the first time, put it right out there. Yes, it may limit your chances, but if you lie at the start, if you aren't honest about something as basic as your age, how can a potential partner trust you? Truth is the foundation of all your relationships. Lies will come back to haunt you. Or as the saying goes, "The truth will set you free!"

While 48 percent of respondents in the ROAR Into survey said they celebrate their age, what about the other half? It's time to wear your age as a badge of honor. It means you have had the good fortune of living longer (and hopefully healthier), assembling the experiences and wisdom you have gathered along the way. What comes with living longer are regrets. In the survey, 46 percent of respondents had relationship regrets, while 39 percent had work regrets. For the forty-five-to-fifty-nine-year-olds, relationship regrets were at 45 percent and 44 percent had work regrets. The examples included everything from not completing college to financial decisions made along the way to being frivolous in their younger years, giving up important building blocks.

A major streak of ageism runs through American culture. Just spend some time looking at the slew of images put forth by marketers, who show couples walking hand in hand into the sunset, almost as if they are heading into the end of their lives. According to research from AARP, more than a third of the US population is older than fifty, yet this demographic represents only 15 percent of media images in advertising.[7] In addition, most of the images are shown at home in the company of a partner or medical professional, instead of showing people over age fifty who are engaging in technology, active sports, or the workplace.

For an industry that prides itself on embracing diversity, it is shameful that this institutionalized ageism exists within the advertising world. Yes, some companies are forward-thinking, including L'Oréal and its spokeswomen. However, positive images of people over fifty are woefully underrepresented: in gender, race, sexual orientation, and religion. It is discrimination that hits everyone. Ask many people over fifty and they will tell you about the experience of "feeling invisible." Our media culture has created that, and it is an inequity that should be confronted by everyone.

Yes, we do have famous role models emerging who are fighting against age stereotypes, such as Jennifer Lopez, who is over fifty, and Bruce Springsteen, who is over seventy, but we need more of them to be front and center. One of my favorite role models has been the singer Sting. Nearly seventy, he exudes charisma, and has a fit physique and a great mind-set. Actress Julianna Margulies said it best: "I like getting older, because I know who I am now. We all do a disservice to try and get it all done when we are young. We have to grow into who we are as we age." (Julianna's story was shared in chapter 1, "Reimagine Your Life Before Others Do It for You.")

More than 50 million people older than fifty are employed, yet they face comments and discrimination in advancement opportunities, as well as in how people respond and react to them. I had my own experience in my company, when an executive who led our digital efforts made comments such as "You know, someone your age . . ." or "When you get to be as old as you are . . ." Finally, after a third comment, I suggested that he not mention my age again or he would hear from my attorney. That shut him up for good. The assumption was that as an older person, I didn't get the digital world, when in fact I not only got it, I led the team to drive tens of millions of dollars of digital advertising revenue.

While companies are finally focused on diversity initiatives, a long-overdue effort, I would also add age as a diversity issue. Too many human resources executives and managers are more interested in how they can find a runway to move older employees out of the workforce than in embracing these employees' experience and wisdom as an integral part of the workforce. For those human resources directors, chief people officers, and hiring managers, it's time to stand up and reinvent how older employees can contribute to your organization's goals. Who are the pioneers out there who will lead this charge? We need a major reckoning on this front.

The same holds true for recruiters at large companies and headhunting firms that have inherent bias within their efforts. They have to stop talking about how sixty-year-olds are unemployable or not eligible for corporate board seats and start acknowledging what incredible expertise and knowledge seasoned professionals bring to a business or organization.

> **ROAR TIP**
>
> If you are fifty or fifty-five or sixty, push for that promotion, that fresh initiative, that advanced training. Only you can shape your destiny with the commitment to learn something new and relevant, keeping your contribution to your company vibrant and your job fulfilling.

I take pride that during my last year as a full-time executive, I promoted a seventy-year-old woman at my company. Carol was not only experienced, she was also one of the most competent publishers I had ever worked with. She drove innovation and embraced up-to-the-minute ideas and trends sooner than many people thirty years younger. My advice to her was to work as long as she wanted to and not to let anyone get in her way.

It is true that certain things are probably not possible at this point in life. You can't become an Olympic athlete at age sixty-five, but you can compete in masters sports. You may not be able to go to medical school at sixty, but you can still enter the health field or expand your horizon in that field. One of my favorite examples is how Dan Tyler,[8] a real estate developer, made his athletic boyhood dream come true in his late forties.

He had always been interested in boxing; he was a student of the sport and his lifelong idol was Muhammad Ali. Dan lives in Miami and was working out at the 5th St. Gym there when he learned that Ali used to work out in the club's separate boxing gym when he was in Miami Beach. Occasionally, Dan would stick his head in to watch the boxers. Soon one of the guys said, "You should come in and have some sparring sessions. Try it out."

ROAR TIP

Make sure you ROAR loudly in the workforce, not taking any pushback from anyone who tries to put a label on you. If it is your goal to stay in the workplace longer, look for people in your company, community, and neighborhood who are thriving at work in their sixties and seventies, and learn from them. Become an activist in your company, industry, and community to dispel the archaic perceptions of older employees.

Hesitant at first, Dan took his first lesson and was hooked. He started to work out in the boxing gym at least three days a week and did more stomach exercises (after he was hit in the stomach and felt that rush of pain go through him) to add strength to his regimen. His trainer continued to encourage him, and one day Dan learned about a charity boxing event at the Magic City Casino in Miami. He committed to training for the tournament in the masters division for people over thirty-five.

Twenty boxers participated in ten fights, and Dan said he felt the electricity in the air. He won his fight by TKO in the third round! Now he was a man on a mission to participate in more boxing matches and to earn his "belt" for the masters. After learning about the Ringside World Championships, he jumped in and competed in 2013 and 2015, making it to the finals. In 2016, he won in his age group at the competition in Kansas City, becoming the world champion!

While he was working on his own boxing career, Dan took his interest in boxing one step further by starting his own company to manage a group of six boxers. He traveled with them to Las Vegas and Detroit, and to Kiev, Ukraine, where one of his boxers competed in front of twenty thousand spectators and went seven rounds, even though he lost in the end.

"I have a passion for the sport . . . the people, the vibe, the culture," Dan said. Now, at fifty-seven, he is much smarter about the sport, and his goal is to work with a boxer who can earn a championship belt. He would also like to get his own second belt, especially since, as he said, the "whole masters thing has exploded on the scene!"

Over the past ten years, as he has pursued his dream, Dan has remained energized. "It changed my life. Something that I didn't think was possible. It just took some courage to take the first step. If you want something so bad, you'll find it."

Another inspiring story is that of Sophia,[9] the daughter of Austrian immigrants. A high school graduate, she had her first child at twenty and a second at twenty-one, and when she was twenty-four, her husband died unexpectedly. She was unsure what her future held when a nun said to her, "You have to get an education." This set her on a course to earn a college degree, despite sometimes having to take her kids to class when she had childcare issues. Ultimately, she became a serial learner. She earned a master's degree in pastoral counseling (marriage and family) and became a clinical social worker. In her late fifties she decided to pursue her original dream of becoming a nurse.

"I wasn't sure I wanted to take on the cost of college tuition, but I found a program with a grant possibility. Even though I had failed chemistry in high school, I decided to go for it," Sophia said. When her state ruled that all new registered professional nurses had to have a bachelor's degree to work in the state, she took her education a step further to earn that additional degree. She'll be ready to hit the nursing job market at sixty-seven. "I'll interview at hospitals and community health centers. I can do research; there are a lot of possibilities," she explained. "I hope to work in this field for the rest of my life."

Sophia knows the importance of moving ahead in a proactive way, as she has worked with older people throughout her life. She's critical of the nursing home system because she believes that it separates the residents from the flow of life, which can lead to atrophy. Her opinion is that there needs to be increased engagement with younger people—perhaps a visit to a college campus once a week for a class—or more contemporary activities, such as working with computers instead of playing bingo.

"People go into despair as they age, often saying, 'I'm too old to do something,' but hope is where you get the energy," she said. Sophia is a role model for living a dynamic life, ROARing into new areas. I suspect we will see her do other interesting things in her seventies and eighties.

Another example of always being proactive in your life is to be open to new love and relationships. Never stop looking for love, as you never know when it might show up on your doorstep. One of my favorite interviews was on NPR. A 107-year-old man and a 100-year-old woman, who were a new couple, were as titillated as if they were high schoolers.[10]

All of us want that intimate connection, regardless of how old we are—and yes, that includes a satisfying sex life. Why should that basic human experience and joy become something that atrophies as we age? Don't we all deserve to have that no matter how old we become? I'm all for people discovering each other at eighty and finding love and intimacy. Actually, by then, we have probably mastered what we want in that part of our lives. If you haven't, it still isn't too late: you're not dead yet! Go and explore your sexual self with a partner, and become fulfilled in what brings you enjoyment.

In the ROAR Into survey, we asked people: *If you had to choose between a wonderful romantic spouse to whom you would be married for only a few years or a boring, unromantic spouse for an entire life, which would you choose?* The answer might surprise you, as a full 50 percent of respondents would choose the romantic spouse, and 31 percent weren't sure (which to me means they were thinking about it!). Interestingly, only 19 percent chose the boring spouse. Long live romance!

For many people over the age of fifty, the idea of online dating is a problem, yet it is how so many people are now meeting new people to date and even to partner with or marry. My friend Chris would line up three coffee dates on a Saturday; my colleague Jayne met a guy who is now her husband; and my friend Steve put his toe in the online dating world and had two hundred women invite him to respond. After two dinner dates and one lunch date over one weekend, he realized that this is not such a bad way to meet people! There are many types of dating sites, with some of them geared to people over fifty: Match, eharmony, SilverSingles, and Zoosk. Spend a few hours identifying the service that works best for you and jump in! As they say, you gotta be in it to win it!

As for children at a later age, there are lots of role models. Journalist Hoda Kotb adopted a child at fifty-two, and singer Janet Jackson gave birth at fifty. I read about a divorced mother of three who met a great guy on a dating site, moved from New York to Michigan to be with him, and became pregnant at fifty-three, with twins![11] If you dream of becoming a parent but haven't found the right partner, there are many role models who have gone it alone. Make your plan, build your support network, and take the leap. Why postpone this joy if it is really what you want?

ROAR TIP

Own the numbers related to your life goals. Are you keeping a tally? For example, if you have a burning desire to travel, make a list. Let's keep it easy: pick one place a year for the next five years. If you stick to the plan, you will accomplish it. Don't let anything get in the way, particularly your own laziness or inertia. If travel is really what you want, get out and do it.

I will admit that I've always been a super goal-oriented person, and that has long been embedded in numbers. I can rattle them all off: 124 countries visited, seven marathons on seven continents, etc. I'm a bit obsessive, but then again, that trait has allowed me to do all the things I set out to do. Too many people I meet say, "Well, I want to start traveling" or "I want to run a 10k." My immediate response is, "What are you waiting for? Let's sit down and plan your trip. Where would you like to go?"

Don't give in to the excuse that you don't have anyone to travel with, because there are now many organizations for single travelers. Better yet, put out a broad net and find friends and acquaintances who feel the same way you do. If your partner is not interested in travel, sit down and explain why it is important to you, and start putting your plans in motion.

When I was turning forty, I decided to have the adventure of climbing Mount Kilimanjaro, the tallest mountain in Africa. Seven of us made the trek, and that was the start of developing my own adventure travel group. Our formula is simple: we are committed to taking at least one adventure together every year, and we plan our destination ahead of time. It's adults only, singles or couples, but our primary criterion is that you cannot be a prima donna, as we are often in places with few creature comforts.

Our group has grown to twenty people, although on any given trip, there are seven or eight of us, based on our schedules and availability. For more than twenty years, we have been to such places as Namibia and Bhutan; we've hiked in Patagonia and Nepal; we've looked for lemurs in Madagascar. Just before the COVID-19 crisis hit, we took an amazing trip to Ethiopia. We all have our adventure funds, and we save our frequent-flier miles to help manage our costs. And we have a long list of what's next, from Western Australia's outback to the John Muir Trail, a long-distance trail in California's Sierra Nevada mountain range. You may not want such an exotic itinerary, but you can certainly start your own group and go to places like Charleston, Santa Fe, and New Orleans, or focus on an activity that you enjoy and make that the center of your trip.

We all know people who talk the talk about wanting to take a road trip across the country or start a business or make a commitment to their health and well-being, but they never seem to get off the ground. I have one friend who is always saying she wants to write a book. It is the cocktail-party chatter that makes her feel good. Once, when I asked her if she had put anything down on paper, she looked a bit stunned. "Well, you've been saying you want to write a book for at least five years, but nothing is happening. Either you should write that book or move on to something else," I said. My comment wasn't meant to hurt her but rather to help her see things more clearly.

I recommended she start a discipline by carving out one hour a day to commit to writing. Maybe she would get into a rhythm, or maybe she would discover that writing that book wasn't what she wanted to do after all. I suggested she pick up a copy of *The Artist's Way* by Julia Cameron. It is an inspirational book that provides insights and techniques on how you can capture your creative talents—to write that book or do whatever endeavor appeals to you.

Another friend would tell anyone who would listen that he was going to run a half marathon. Yet he never trained for it or decided on when he might do it. Finally, I had to say, "Admit it, you are not going to run a half marathon. It sounds good, but it isn't happening." I suggested he start by running a 5k to get the hang of running a race, then move up to a 10k, and then decide if he still wanted to tackle a half marathon. Too many people talk about what they think they want to do, instead of actually doing it.

ROAR TIP

It might sound harsh to tell your friends or family that they're merely talking about a goal, not actually doing anything about it. I believe this is an energizing way to nudge people into real action. And we need to do the same with ourselves. How many times have we had something on our own goal list that we just never get to? Either we have to shed it from the list or start doing it. Push yourself out of the inertia that has taken over your life. My formula is simple: write what it is that you want to do, and book it like an appointment.

Think big, too! Let's say you have always wanted to go on an African safari. At first, it might seem daunting to even start, but it is not as hard as you think. A one-hour online search will help you find companies that are experts in the area, specific ones that cater to seniors and make cost comparisons, such as Tripadvisor and other review sites. Put the word out to your friends or on your social media of choice that you want to go to Africa, and ask if anyone can help you. Within days, you'll have resources that will help you formulate your plan. The information or support you're looking for is right at your fingertips, so there's no real excuse. Make the commitment to what you want to do, and stick with it.

I'm a big believer that you should have a grand adventure for your big birthdays. At fifty, I went to Antarctica to conquer my seventh continent and one hundredth country visited. At sixty, I went back to Antarctica to run a marathon, so you might say it doesn't get more adventurous than that. When I turn seventy, I'm hoping to do the Tenzing Hillary Everest Marathon, which entails a hike to the Everest Base Camp and a marathon run down. While it is still a few years away, I'm planning for it today.

I'm even thinking about what I'll do at eighty. Assuming that adventure marathons may be in my past, I hope to celebrate by doing what's known as Wainwright's Coast-to-Coast walk in Northern England, a 182-mile long-distance footpath through the Lake District, Yorkshire Dales, and North York Moors national parks. Who knows what my life will be like at eighty? But right now it is in my mind that this is what I want to experience—with, I hope, some family and friends in tow.

ROAR TIP

Own your ultimate number. Face it: you're going to die; we all do. You can ignore it all you want, be fearful about it, or deny it, but it is our common shared experience. So, why not lean into it? Think about it and start planning for it in all of its various dimensions. I have to admit that I am an avid reader of obituaries. They are mini-biographies, summing up a person's life in a way that tells you what made them special. Here's a challenge: write your own obituary now. Ask yourself: *What do I want the world to know about me? What was my legacy to my family, friends, and community?* It's a helpful exercise to see if you are actually living the life you want to live.

I'm always shocked to learn that a friend doesn't have a will, a power of attorney or health, or a living will. It's true that it won't be that person's problem after death, but that is a selfish attitude, as people who care about them will be forced to deal with their irresponsibility. So, what are your true wishes? Do you want a do-not-resuscitate agreement, or do you want to be kept alive by any and all means? Do you want to be buried or cremated? Would you prefer a solemn remembrance ceremony, or do you want a party to celebrate your life? My advice is to make these decisions clear to your family and friends. I also recommend writing your own eulogy and designating someone to read it to those who come out to remember you. Tell the world what you learned and what you want them to know as your legacy and your contribution to everyone.

Death was something I learned about at a young age, because my grandfather was an undertaker. He had a small family-run business serving the immigrant community on the south side of Pittsburgh. As a kid, I did odd jobs around the funeral home, later on joining my grandfather to pick up bodies; I also watched him embalm them and prepare for the rituals of viewing and burial. I learned a lot by observing the American way of dying in those days, but most important, these experiences gave me perspective on death.

I witnessed the grief from families, yet it always surprised me when family members would show up to pay their respects after years of estrangement, and then disappear again from the family members affected. What is that all about? Death brings out a lot in families: pain and sadness, certainly, but also greed about inheritances and money.

ROAR TIP

The only way you can take care of your family after you are gone is to be clear about your wishes in regard to what you want to leave them. And here's a hint: In your will, state explicitly that if anyone challenges your wishes, that person will get nothing. It is a clause that works and has been proven in court. Consult with your attorney on how to incorporate this into your final will.

I also believe in the "die broke" philosophy. (In fact, there's a book written with that very title by Stephen M. Pollan and Mark Levine.) If you love your family, take care of them while you are alive. Pay for educations, take the grandkids on trips, help with a mortgage. Help your family members to improve their lives while you are alive. What is this obsession we have with leaving wealth for our heirs? Have enough to pay for your own desired burial, and leave this earth clear of any potential infighting that can tear families apart. Not to mention what might be owed in taxes! Also, plan for ways that you will support your favorite charities, a topic I'll address in chapter 12, "Reassess Your Community and Your Relationship with It."

Better yet, spend most of your money on yourself. You earned it, so why not enjoy it? While some people may say that is selfish, I would argue, why? If you are providing all that you, your partner, and your family need, then you are fulfilling your responsibility. Go have some fun. Indulge yourself with what matters to you.

It's true that most people have some anxiety about financial security, especially as we all live longer lives. That's why owning your financial number and your age number is important, along with your ultimate number.

What if you worry that you will run out of money or live on a meager income once you hit eighty? Well, the question is, "What are you going to do about it now?" Talk to your children or relatives about your concerns to see if they will help out. Get a part-time job. Take a reverse mortgage. Sell things that no longer matter to you. Spend an hour or two Googling "how do I make sure I don't run out of money in retirement?" You will find helpful tips from myriad sources. But unless and until you have identified your own numbers, you won't have a clear view of your future needs, so how can you make a plan for the rest of your life?

Embrace that you will be leaving this earth and prepare for it on the health, wealth, and spiritual fronts.

Embrace that you will be leaving this earth and prepare for it on the health, wealth, and spiritual fronts. Also, be realistic: your partner might die before you do. Have you had the conversation about your combined financial situation, health proxy, and personal wishes after death? As important, have you thought about what you might do if you find yourself alone? It's okay to visualize how you will carry on. It might be painful, but it should be part of your personal future. Will you stay in the same house? Move to another state? Start dating again? Sketching out the possibilities is healthy, as is discussing it with your mate.

ROAR TIP

We all hope we will live to an ultimate number that is a big number, but there are no guarantees. Are you ready for your last day? It could happen in a day, a week, or a year. Can you say that you lived a life you are proud of and can leave, having acknowledged that?

When I've talked to older people who have a more realistic perspective on death, it is always enlightening to see who has done the mental work to accept that we all eventually die. In his *New York Times* essay, "What Is Death?," hospice and palliative medicine physician BJ Miller wrote a profound statement that has stuck with me since I read it: "Death is the force that shows you what you love and urges you to revel in that love while the clock ticks."[12] Do you want to have achieved that and to have peace at your life's end? Spend some time thinking about this so that you can ROAR into the next life, whatever you believe it holds.

ROAR: Chapter Takeaways

- Your numbers help to define your well-being. The biological part of you is your own unique set of stats. Keep tabs on your blood pressure, heart rate, cholesterol. Your numbers are the road map to a long and healthy life. And with medical histories in digital format now, it's much easier to keep tabs on your health facts.

- Your financial security is in your hands. Manage "smart debt" and pay yourself first through a 401(k) or other savings. Do you have a traditional pension? What is your calculated Social Security payout at various ages? What's your net worth number right now? Are you happy with where you are and where you are going? Work your numbers!

- Age doesn't mean anything anymore. If you are fifty, you have reached a milestone! Every year is a gift. Celebrate it and flex those wisdom-and-experience muscles to accomplish even more. Better yet, share that wisdom with your loved ones or as a mentor to others.

- You can't realize your goals unless you write them down and monitor your own progress. If you have spent a whole year and haven't moved any of them forward, you only have yourself to blame. Have a monthly check-in on your goals. If the same ones keep showing up and nothing has happened, ask yourself why.
- We may want to ignore it, deny it, or fight it, but we are all going to die. Your mission should be finding peace with it now and shaping the rest of your life. How do you want to be remembered? Write your own eulogy and read it to yourself. Are you the person you set out to be? If not, make the time you have right now count!

5

Own Your Wins, Strengths, Opportunities, and Successes

Success is loving life and daring to live it.
—Maya Angelou

When asked how I get so much done, I respond by saying that it is all about the SWOT: strengths, weaknesses, opportunities, and threats. It's been a life formula for my professional and personal life—and it can work for you too. But the only way to make it effective is if you are completely honest with yourself about what you are good at and what you are not good at. Also, you have to be aware of every opportunity that comes your way and jump into it, as well as know the things that stand in your way and how to overcome them.

> *You have to be aware of every opportunity that comes your way and jump into it, as well as know the things that stand in your way and how to overcome them.*

For those of you who have studied business, the SWOT analysis, which was developed by Albert S. Humphrey at the Stanford Research Institute, is a tool that you might have learned, allowing you to identify strengths, weaknesses, opportunities, and threats for your company. It is often used in the beginning of a decision-making process to build out a strategic plan for the goals desired. It's also a great approach to take in your own life:

- **Strengths.** You know your innate or learned skills. What are you good at? Are you the one people turn to for a shoulder to lean on, recognizing your compassion? Are you a financial whiz who dispenses advice to your family and friends? Do you know more about biology and health than anyone in your extended group? All of these qualities make you the unique individual that you are.

- **Weaknesses.** We all have them. In your own mind, you know your weaknesses and how you have to rely on help to get you through an issue. Although I can read a profit-and-loss statement and have a great grasp of financial reports, I'm lousy at math in general. Sometimes I can be uncoordinated, so I've leaned into athletic endeavors that don't rely on that, like running, hiking, and kayaking, although I love to ski, a sport that requires coordinated moves. I have a friend who admits to having poor coping skills when life throws him a curveball. I admire his acknowledgment of that weakness and how he is working on changing that.

- **Opportunities.** With all your strengths and experiences, how can you tap into opportunities that will enhance your position in life? Have you carved out a unique skill through your work—for example, data analytics that will allow you to excel in this rapidly growing field? Or have you identified a desirable skill as an area of growth and planned to do some adult education to develop it? Education institutions around the country have exploded with certificate programs and master's degrees in a wide range of areas, from real estate development to niche programs that can spin you off into a new direction. And don't rule out the trades: we need more plumbers and electricians and carpenters. Learn more about what interests you. Also, this isn't only about work. If you are single and looking for a new partner and have a honed skill such as sailing, spend time at your local waterway to meet other like-minded people. It's where an opportunity might present itself.

- **Threats.** Like competitors that are doing better than your company, there are always issues that will encroach on your well-being.

What are they? A chronic health problem? An industry that is in fast decline? A partner who has lost interest in you? Prioritize handling the threats that matter most to you, and then start the process of figuring out how you will manage them.

So how do you analyze your SWOT qualities? There are tests, quizzes, and approaches that can help you identify what you are best at and what you are not so great at. By the time you hit your mid-forties, you should have a handle on that, but everyone can benefit from a refresher course. The Myers-Briggs Type Indicator (MBTI) is one resource that helps you identify how you take in information and assess your decision-making skills. Another is the RichardStep Strengths and Weaknesses Aptitude Test (RSWAT), and there are many more. You can spend a whole weekend scouring the internet and taking multiple tests to see if the findings match up!

ROAR TIP

Take out a piece of paper and do your own SWOT analysis. And be brutally honest with yourself; you know who you are. You should also get feedback from other people: What do they say you are good at? What do they compliment you on? I know that one of my strengths is to motivate people to do their best, and that I excel at speaking to groups, small and large. I also know that one of my weaknesses is not being that mechanical, like repairing a lawn mower or figuring out why the grill is not working. Fortunately, one of my strengths is knowing who to call for help!

In the ROAR Into survey, only 31 percent of the respondents claimed that they always leverage their strengths, and only 24 percent of those between ages sixty and seventy-five claimed that they do so—a group of people who should have a pretty strong understanding of their strengths at that point in their life. It's the same with celebrating wins and success. Only 37 percent responded that they always celebrate them, and 40 percent claim that they feel complacent about their achievements because they have lived with them for so long. C'mon, people! If you don't have a clear appreciation and celebration for what you are best at, then how can you maximize the way to build on it? So, take time to acknowledge your strengths and successes—celebrate!

I've always believed that when an opportunity shows up, you have to pounce on it—if it is right for you. It happens every day—the possibility of a new job, a new love, a new place to live. You know when an opportunity is right for you at a given time. One of my best-loved stories is about a friend's mother, who was divorced. She and a group of friends bought season passes to the opera, but at one point, most of them decided not to renew, so she bought a ticket on her own. At that point, she was sixty-two years old and had been single for thirty years. A seventy-three-year-old widower bought the seat next to her and struck up a conversation. They've been married for twenty years. She is eighty-two and he is ninety-three! You just never know what might happen at a night at the opera, the ballpark, or the theater.

> **ROAR TIP**
>
> We all have some kind of creative gene in us. I would make a lousy painter or sculptor (I've tried), but I feel comfortable writing and producing photography. Lean into that creative gene and be expansive in how you think about it. If you have frequently been told you're a great musician, what are you going to do about it? Everyone has something that might allow them to express themselves creatively and leverage a dormant strength.

We all love hearing stories like that. The people who meet on a bus and have a coffee that leads to a romance, or the lost love who reappears when you are visiting a museum and the relationship is rekindled. They may all be serendipity moments, yet they are also opportunities for wins and successes that you didn't imagine could happen. But you can't dilly-dally around, whether in your personal life or your professional life. Jump in and see where opportunity takes you, especially as you get older: time is running out!

One of my favorite stories about opportunity is also about one of my favorite people—Erik Logan.[1] I'm always drawn to positive, dynamic personalities, and he is one of those. Born in Oklahoma City, Erik said his early claim to fame was being "Chuck the Duck" and "Cody the Coyote" when he was a teenager, dressing up as those characters to pass out coupons on the street and promote local radio stations. In fact, he fell in love with radio, working as a high school deejay and working in radio at college. But he was restless, and he left college with no degree to step into the radio world full-time.

He knew his strengths in the medium, and in fast succession, he became a program director at twenty, launched a new country station in Seattle at twenty-two, and ran a station in the San Francisco market before relocating to Tampa Bay. Eventually Erik moved to Chicago for a bigger job, and then to New York to be vice president at CBS Radio. All this before he was in his early thirties. Talk about maximizing his wins and successes and leaping into new opportunities!

But then when he was in his mid-thirties, something happened in his industry called "satellite radio." He got a call to interview with this newly emerging approach, but he was skeptical about its future. Nevertheless, he drove down to Washington, DC, to have a conversation with the company, and two facts struck him. First of all, using satellite radio he didn't have to change stations on the ride down, and there were no commercials during his four-hour drive! When he got there, he was given a tour of stunning offices with the various stations all right down the hall from each other. It dawned on him: "This was the future, right in front of me," he said, as he decided to jump in. The experience was a whirlwind, from building the business and audience to creating niche stations with everything from Dr. Oz to Spanish soccer to the *Oprah & Friends* (later branded *Oprah Radio*) channel.

Flash-forward. Oprah called. Another opportunity. Erik then spent nine years at OWN, the Oprah Winfrey Network (where I met him), ultimately becoming president of OWN and HARPO, Oprah's multimedia production company. Wins and successes. But his story gets even better.

When OWN moved to Los Angeles, Erik and his family moved to the West Coast and chose to settle in Manhattan Beach to be close to his parents, who had moved there. "It was an interesting choice because I don't like seafood or boats or the ocean. In fact, my wife bought me a wetsuit as a gag gift, and I put it on backwards," he joked. Then one day when he was in his early forties, he put on the wetsuit and went into the ocean just to see what it was like. "All I can say is that it was one of the most powerful emotions I had ever felt. Being in the ocean was a transformative moment, and in a split second, I lost the ingrained fear that I had had of the ocean," he told me.

That one small step into the water changed his life. He started taking surfing lessons. After all, if the Pacific Ocean is right in front of you, why not? "Riding a wave is like harnessing raw energy. You have to leave your ego on the beach, as you become one with the board beneath your feet," Erik said, laughing. Surfing unlocked the world for him, as he took trips to Fiji and Costa Rica and fell in love with how Mother Nature handles the oceans.

Ultimately, he invested in a local surf shop, then a surfboard company, and then a venture with Laird Hamilton, one of the top surfers in the world. You might say that Erik dove into the deep end and rode his passion. That energy led him to move deeper into the surf world, as he learned more about the players and what made the industry tick. Then, as life happens, another opportunity appeared in front of him: to get involved in the World Surf League, the governing body for professional surfers. He became an advisor, and then he was presented with an opportunity to become the league's president of content, media, and studios. In 2019, Erik became CEO of the World Surf League.

How do you leave Oprah Winfrey, you might ask?

"'You have found your spiritual calling,' Oprah told me, when I sat down to talk about the opportunity," he explained. Deciding whether to move on was a four-month process, with a lot of soul-searching, as well as many discussions with his wife and best friend. "This career path found me. It was an opportunity that presented itself, and I knew that I had to step in." Now fifty years old, Erik is living, in Oprah's words, "his best life."

What's the lesson? Erik always appreciated his wins and successes and believed in leveraging his strengths: first his love of radio, then media, and then surfing. He took every opportunity that came his way and would tell you that there were tough times along the way, but they never stopped him from moving forward. The boy from Oklahoma City with no college degree and a sheer love of living continues to ROAR. He and I will always be friends, and I cannot wait to see what he does in the decades ahead!

> **ROAR TIP**
>
> Don't ever stop chasing your dreams, especially the ones that show up in your forties and fifties and beyond. ROAR into them!

We all know people who have a glass half full versus those with a glass half empty. And then there are those whose glass spills over: those are my kind of people. Surround yourself with them, as their glow will bring sunlight into your life.

Under the headline that most people are optimistic, 67 percent of the respondents in the ROAR Into survey said that there is still so much more they want to achieve in their life. For those age sixty to seventy-five, the response was 62 percent. However, 54 percent said, "There are so many dreams that I have but just haven't gotten to them yet!" How about getting started today?

In order to have personal or professional wins and successes, you need some type of plan. In the survey, 46 percent said they do not have a concrete plan for the future. If you are like that 46 percent, take pen to paper and start writing down how you see your life progressing. If you have no idea where to start, that unto itself is a good start. By acknowledging that you want a future of new opportunities and successes, you will begin the journey.

Jeanne Marin (Jeanne Franck, MD)[2] started working on her plan while she was a well-known and respected dermatologist specializing in Mohs micrographic surgery and cutaneous oncology, a special technique used to treat skin cancer. At fifty-five—after thirty years as a physician (twenty-five of them as a dermatologist)—she assessed her success and her strengths and decided to become a veterinarian!

"I always loved science, and I've had great success and recognition, but I'm passionate about how I can make a difference in a different way without peer reviews. I always knew that I wanted to do something for the dogs in our world," Jeanne explained. After thinking about the horror of puppy mills and the overpopulation of dogs, among other issues, she considered this life change seriously for about a year.

When she read that a local university had just received state approval for a new veterinary school, she applied for the four-year program, and she was accepted. Jeanne's goal is to become an "activist veterinarian," joining up with a nonprofit or even creating her own to tackle some of the issues facing our four-legged friends and their owners. She'll continue to work as a dermatologist, but she'll pull back on her operation and the hours put in, so that she can eventually transition into her new life as she approaches sixty years old. "This new career might be shorter, but who knows?" she said.

ROAR TIP

Don't get stuck on autopilot. It will put you in a suspended state of inertia. Take the controls, flip the switch, and live an awakened life!

While Erik and Jeanne are examples of high achievers who owned their successes and strengths to step into new opportunities, it can be done at any level. My sister Peg was a fitness trainer who leveraged that experience to launch a spinning studio. A local neighbor who started a lawn-mowing business now has a major landscaping company. He leveraged the client relationships to start expanding his offerings, taking on every opportunity he could.

Countless people have "woken up" and taken charge of their lives, creating new and exciting chapters that have brought them enormous fulfillment. At fifty-eight, David Massey was unhappy with the management of the company he worked for and decided it was time to leave. He had bought some land in northern Minnesota and thought he'd try his hand at organic farming. Some ten years later, Farmer Dave, as he is known by the locals, has turned eight acres into a paradise of fruits and vegetables, including over sixty types of heirloom tomatoes, twenty kinds of potatoes, and multiple varieties of kale, blueberries, squash, and more. David (a chemist by training) and his wife, Pam Tasker, operate Northwoods Organic Produce, where they take pride in using environmentally friendly growing techniques that promote disease resistance and healthy soil for their various seed productions.[3] He's become a local celebrity, along with providing his community with a unique food source.[4]

Traci Blackstock worked as an office manager for a dog-training company. She had always had a knack for fixing things, an innate skill she thought she should develop. She just needed to figure out how she might do that. In her early fifties, a visit to her local Home Depot made her realize that there was her answer, in her own backyard. After thinking through how she might fit in at Home Depot, she put together a resume and started the process of approaching the store's management for a role there. Today, she works full-time in the tool-rental department and says that for the first time, she is doing what she truly loves.[5]

Stories abound of folks like Dave and Traci, who turned their innate skills into opportunities. An administrative assistant who learned the art of flower arranging and became the local go-to person for special occasions. A guy stuck in a no-future office job, who chased his love of tinkering with cars and became the neighborhood expert on car repair. All it takes is figuring out what you truly like to do and then using your imagination to create how you step forward into a new life purpose.

Riccardo Orizio,[6] a journalist by trade, is a bold thinker and a bold doer. In his forties, after listening to many people's stories, he had a revelation. He said he was "terrified that dreams and ambitions would be covered with the debris of a normal career." He had already led an exciting life as a foreign correspondent for Italian media, covering conflicts in various parts of the world, but something was nagging at him. "I always had a bit of a wild side inside myself," he told me, as he decided that he would pick up and move to Africa. He had some connections in Kenya and had been there a few times, but now he wanted to make it home, as he always felt a kinship when he visited there.

In the beginning, Riccardo lived in the bush, based in the Masai Mara. He slowly built his credibility, understanding and working within the Masai and Samburu communities with the idea of somehow creating a place that would bring cultures together. Flash-forward seventeen years. He now owns four safari lodges—two in Samburu (northern

Kenya) and two in the Masai Mara (in the south)—under the name Saruni: a collection of lodges in private wildlife conservancies in cooperation with local communities. This new model is an innovative way to give value to the land owned by communities, and at the same time, create unique experiences for visitors. When I asked Riccardo what his advice would be for someone taking such a big, unknown leap like he did, his response was, "Always balance your heart and your mind. If you only listen to your mind, you never do it. If you only use your heart, you risk doing it badly."

Obviously, a lot happened from his arrival in Kenya to where he is today, something that could fill a book! My suggestion to Riccardo, already an author of several books, was that he should tell all of us the tale of how he created his life in Kenya. I'm sure it would be an inspiring read.

On the subject of inspiring, London resident Eugene Hughes[7] has created a business specially built for those interested in pursuing their own personal ROAR. During a successful career in global management consulting, Eugene began to realize that the corporate life never comfortably fit him. "A coat too tight," he explained. Yet he was trapped by his own success, doing what he called the survival dance, not his soul dance. One day a colleague asked him, "What are you really hungry for?" and it set him on to an awakening that changed his life's direction.

Eugene had always been interested in how his connection to nature allowed him to discover himself. He also wanted to learn more about the human psyche, which led him to start studying psychology, including Gestalt therapy, psychoanalytic art, and psychotherapy. In his mid-forties he qualified to become a psychotherapist and found a unique niche for people over forty who were questioning their lives. By combining his love of psychology and nature, Eugene's company, Artgym, takes people into the wilderness to "meet themselves."

"Our clients are people who are at the point of asking, what now?" he told me, adding that the goal is to help people identify what is their authentic contribution to the world. By combining wilderness survival tools and psychotherapeutic techniques, eight-day experiences in places such as the Atlas Mountains in Morocco help people separate from their everyday lives and learn how to be on their own in nature. "Nature shapes our relationship with ourselves," he said. Eugene noted that in his mid-fifties, he is definitely doing his life's work, helping people to uncover how they are stuck and guiding them to what's next. And this is how he plans to spend the rest of his life.

The preceding success stories are a result of vision, drive, and ambition, along with knowing what you are and are not good at. And, I would add, listening to your heart. As Riccardo Orizio said, "Always balance your heart and your mind."

If you feel stuck, that the right opportunities are not happening, then you need to create your own.

As for opportunities, they are there for you every day in all parts of your life. Not only do you have to be aware of them, but you need to move swiftly on them. I like to call this the "harmonic convergence," when all the planets seem aligned and the universe is telling you that what is in front of you is right for you, and you should act on it. If you feel stuck, that the right opportunities are not happening, then you need to create your own. Never be satisfied until you find the right company, the right job, the right partner, or the right lifestyle.

In the ROAR Into survey, 40 percent of respondents said they tend to "go through life on autopilot," and 41 percent said, "I find myself saying 'I'm too old to do that,' whether it's about a career change, a job change, travel, or anything else I want to do."

Those are all self-imposed traps, excuses that hold you back from your own growth and happiness.

ROAR: Chapter Takeaways

- Know your SWOT: your strengths, weaknesses, opportunities, and threats. Recognize that these are always changing as you learn more, as the world changes around you, and as new opportunities come your way. It's all what makes you an exciting individual.
- If you are a bit lost, spend some time doing the Myers-Briggs Type Indicator test or the RichardStep Strengths and Weaknesses

Aptitude Test (RSWAT). These are two examples of ways to help you focus.

- Every one of us has a creative gene that needs to be expressed. It might be rooted in your childhood or discovered later in life. Nurture it. Grow it. Let it become the natural extension of who you are. It can also be your lifelong pursuit.

- Every day, new opportunities present themselves to you—in work, life, love, lifestyle. You know when the right one presents itself. Seize the moment and take the opportunity that is right for you.

- Role models are all around you, people who have changed it up and are thriving. Learn from their stories. Be inspired by them, ask them for advice and support. Make your moves, and then pay it forward.

6

Own Your Losses, Weaknesses, Failures, and Threats

> Every now and then, bite off more than you can chew.
> —Kobi Yamada

et's be honest, we have all lost or failed at something that was important to us, whether it was a job, a relationship, or an endeavor of some other kind. It's just part of the human condition. How you integrate losses and failures into your life makes you the person you become. There will be more losses and failures ahead, so embrace that fact and build the skills that will help you persevere and navigate those choppy waters when they arrive.

How you integrate losses and failures into your life makes you the person you become.

Randy Boyd[1] knows a lot about business cycles. The founder of Radio Systems Corporation and PetSafe, which together produce more than 4,600 technology-based pet products (including Invisible Fence), he can tell you about how he had to close his first company after six months due to a lack of reorders. He can also explain how the 2008 recession hit his business hard and how new product development sometimes failed due to quality problems.

"Anyone who is successful has had a failure along the way," he told me. "The key is to be persistent and always persevere." In 2020, Randy sold his company to a major private equity firm, capping twenty-nine years of being in business. But his story doesn't end there.

The first person in his family to go to college (University of Tennessee), Randy always had an interest in helping those who were threatened by not having a great future. In 2013, as an unpaid advisor to Governor Bill Haslam of Tennessee, he launched the Drive to 55 initiative, which included the Tennessee Promise and Tennessee Reconnect. Together, these programs have helped over four hundred thousand Tennesseans—from high schoolers to older adults—attend community or technical college, tuition-free.[2] But he didn't stop there. He went on to be the unpaid commissioner of economic and community development for the state, handing the reins of his company to his COO, as Randy became executive chair. In 2017, he ran for governor and lost—a failure that he took in stride.

However, one of his friends and supporters asked if he would be interested in becoming the interim president of the University of Tennessee, an idea that he loved, since he is passionate about higher education. He accepted, and during that interim, he established the UT Promise scholarship and mentoring program, which provides free tuition for Tennessee residents whose annual family household income is below $50,000. Randy provided an amazing opportunity for those who might be weak economically. In March 2020, at age sixty, he was appointed president for a term of five years, overseeing the statewide university system of fifty-two thousand students and a staff of fifteen thousand![3] And he did it for no salary![4]

His story still doesn't end there. He relayed that he and his wife, Jenny, have become major philanthropists, donating millions to more than a hundred charities. Through his journey, Randy took any losses and failures as part of life, always adding to his experience and giving back. "We all gain a tremendous amount of experience and wisdom in our lives. Don't be afraid to leverage your skills into another area," he said, adding that his desires to do good and make the world a bit better are what drive him. He plans to stay in public service for the rest of his life and acknowledges that years of hard work put him in the position to do that. Clearly, Randy has many more chapters ahead of him.

Not everyone will have a story as incredible as Randy's, but certainly we have all had losses and failures along the way, with the hope that the wins and successes outweigh those tough periods. A failure might be something as simple as failing a course, as I did in college. Calculus was hard for me, and I think I just gave in during the term. Yet I had to figure out how to take it again and pass, which I did during a summer session after hiring a tutor. I told myself that I was getting in my own way with the barrier I had put up—the belief that I couldn't "get" calculus. Once I adopted the right mind-set, I was able to learn the concepts behind differential and integral calculus, and I actually enjoyed the work (well, almost).

Over the years, I've lost numerous business deals to competitors. Although at one point I took that personally, eventually I realized that it is just the way the world works. We can't win all the time, even though we strive for it. Failure is part of the human experience, and once you are in midlife, you begin to realize that acknowledging those failures may in fact empower you to be stronger and better and more successful. In other words, wear them as a badge of honor. I keep a list of all my failures and losses. I promise myself not to dwell on them but rather to use them as life lessons that taught me something.

Listening to other people's failures can be inspiring, particularly when they find a new direction out of the adversity. Every school should offer a course about failure and how to embrace it, manage it, and turn it into a next opportunity. In the ROAR Into survey, 43 percent of respondents said they tend to dwell on their mistakes and rehash them; only 24 percent strongly agree that they own their insecurities.

How do we embrace loss, whether it is being fired from a job, getting a divorce, or dealing with an impending threat such as a job reorganization that is staring you in the face? How do we confront our own weaknesses?

In my family, we have a lot of addiction, mostly alcohol. My father has been sober for over forty-two years. My sister and brother are sober. It has already moved into the next generation, but my nephew has been sober for over five years. Alcoholism is in our family history, and it is something that we talk about, especially with the younger generation. It's an inherent weakness, as we are genetically predisposed to it.

The only way to confront a weakness is to acknowledge it. Put it front and center and decide if you are going to deal with it or not. Only the individual can make that decision; you can't blame or rely on anyone else. Confronting alcoholism or any addiction takes enormous courage and stamina to stay the course, and I have great respect for people who can proudly count the days and weeks and years of their sobriety.

Of course, weaknesses come in all forms: fear of rejection, lack of confidence, consistent pessimism. The list can go on and on, but only you can identify your weaknesses and how to start to address them. Identify and face your weaknesses one at a time, then begin challenging your preconceived idea of each weakness. One way to do this is by putting another lens on what you think is a weakness and seeing that it is actually the opposite.

Here's an example. My friend Jennifer is an enormously successful fundraiser for a nonprofit organization. People are always amazed at what she can deliver on. In a conversation, she was appalled when I said to her, "You would be amazing in sales at a for-profit company." She went on and on about how she could never do sales effectively and how she hated the idea of sales. I suggested to her that when she was fundraising, she was actually selling—pitching donors and foundations and government organizations for support. A perceived weakness was actually a strength.

ROAR TIP

Take your weakness and turn it inside out. Why do you think it is a weakness? Is it because in high school you hated algebra, so you have labeled yourself math phobic ever since? There are courses and coaches and friends who can help you home in on a weakness and get to the core of it. You might find that what you thought was a weakness actually isn't, but if it is a true weakness, then at least you can acknowledge and manage it.

Surrounding yourself with smart people who can help you has always been one of the great lessons for business success. You can do that in your personal life, too. I always love people who acknowledge their losses and failures, as they put it right out there. They are the ones who have dealt with it and have moved forward. Their stories are life lessons for all of us.

Colleen Daly[5] has a great story about how she found a successful new life out of a loss. We met when she was executive director of the Community Library in Ketchum, Idaho, which she turned into a dynamic center for cultural programming, in addition to serving the community with traditional library offerings. She had dropped out of college to move to Idaho to live the outdoor lifestyle, and had married and made the decision not to have children.

At fifty-four, Colleen was divorced and enjoying life in that beautiful part of the world. She was also working as a book editor and writing coach on the side to augment her income. Through a recommendation, someone from the American Academy in Rome's New York office reached out to see if she might be interested in their job opening for a director of development. She'd always had New York in the back of her mind; she had many friends there and had visited often. In addition, she loved all things Italian and spoke Italian, a language she had studied for years. It so happened that she was going to be in New York, so she scheduled an interview. She thought there was no way she was going to get the job, but she didn't want to look back in a few years and wish she'd given it a shot.

Several weeks later, her interviewer called to let her know she was a serious candidate. Shortly thereafter, she received an offer to join the Academy. "I was ready for the big time, totally gung-ho," she said. Then one of her best friends said to her, "They are going to chew you up and spit you out!" Colleen admitted that her feelings were hurt, but she ignored her friend's words and said to herself, "I'm going to live the rest of my life in the center of the universe!" She put her Idaho apartment on the market, sold her car and furnishings, and moved east.

Her entry into New York went smoothly. She found an apartment, connected with friends, and worked the typical New Yorker schedule of ten hours or more a day as she jumped into the job. However, she was paying a New York rent on top of the mortgage on her Ketchum condo that wasn't selling—a serious financial burden. About a year into the job, she realized it wasn't working. "I wasn't happy, and they weren't happy. We both realized it wasn't a good fit," she said. She had reached the moment when she had to decide what to do.

Totally by chance, an old family friend had connected her to his friend in Washington, DC, an accomplished senior administrator at a major museum. When this friend of a friend came to New York, he was able to lend an ear on what might be next for Colleen. She left the Academy job with the idea of finding a new job in New York. At this time, she reactivated her book editing business to tide her over, since she was down to the end of her savings.

Simultaneously, she and Dodge, her new Washington friend, a widower, realized there were sparks flying between them, and soon they were officially dating. During that summer, Dodge invited her to move to Washington, and once again she had to decide what to do. Should she stay in New York, where the job prospects weren't panning out? Move back to Idaho, since she had already shipped most of her possessions there? Or should she think about moving to Washington, DC?

Colleen decided to give Washington a try. That was more than seven years ago now. She and Dodge are happily married. They travel and enjoy the cultural world, reading and attending lectures. At sixty-three, Colleen is back in business as a book editor and writing coach. She has also found herself part of a large family with Dodge's daughters and four grandchildren.

Life can work in funny ways when you are faced with a loss or a failure. Out of nowhere a new possibility presents itself. When I asked Colleen if she thought it was a risk to move to Washington, her response was, "I've been lucky. My confidence has always been born out of my friends who have enabled me to make pivots in my life." Ultimately, the decision to move was an easy one, as she had fallen in love, something that she wasn't necessarily expecting to happen at that point in her life.

Sometimes you can foresee the loss of a job or that your company isn't going to survive, and it poses a major threat to your livelihood and your future. It happens with established executives, everyday workers, teachers, and more. In that case, the failure is not yours, but the road ahead is your responsibility.

Michael Kassan[6] is one such story. Michael is a bit of a force. A lawyer by training, he had moved into the media agency world, where advertising is bought from major companies in television, print, out-door, and radio. Digital hadn't been relevant in the days when he headed up one of the largest independent media agencies in the country. As president and CEO of the agency, Michael led the initiative to sell the business to one of the industry's major holding companies. After the sale, in his early fifties, he found himself out of a job when he and one of the senior leaders disagreed on the direction of the company.

"At that point, I decided I didn't want to be a media guy who knew what used to happen in the space; I wanted to understand what is going to happen," he explained. As part of his exit agreement, he had an eighteen-month noncompete, so he decided to jump into learning all things digital, as it was beginning to be a serious force in the world. Plus, he told me, he wanted to be relevant to his kids.

He wondered if he would ever get another job, as being unemployed in your fifties can be a bit treacherous, but he wanted to stay involved. His solution? He started his own company, christened MediaLink, a media consulting business that would help companies understand what the trends were in the industry. He then began to work his contacts.

Michael is known as an über-connector, always bringing people together for opportunities, deals, and even jobs. He had begun from the ground up, and at this point in his mid-fifties, things were clicking. A major turning point was when he got a strategic assignment for Disney, which then led to other projects for major entertainment, media, and agency clients. When he was fifty-nine, the business was humming along so well that he even had some interest in companies acquiring the firm. But, as his wife, Ronnie, advised him, "Why would you sell? You are just starting, and it is growing, and you are enjoying yourself!"

Over the next decade, Michael and his team became a major power in the media world, growing to almost two hundred employees with global assignments that kept them busy in lots of relevant areas. In 2017, he finally said it was time to sell, and in his late sixties, he sold the company for $207 million.

"I would never have been smart enough to build a business plan that got me there," he laughed, acknowledging that it was old-fashioned hard work and hustle that brought him to that place. Now as he approaches seventy, he continues to run the company under its parent company.

He's out meeting clients, connecting people, and being the force that he is. For him, success is about staying connected and relevant. With all the chaos in the media world, he believes he can play a role for years to come. Michael's lesson stemmed from being unemployed: He moved forward despite the looming threat of failure in his new venture. He persevered and continues to ROAR.

> **ROAR TIP**
>
> When a door closes, follow your heart and a window will open. Sometimes you just have to go with your instinct. Don't overthink it.

One of my favorite stories is about Paul Pakusch,[7] who lives in upstate New York. After thirty-two years working at local television stations in the control room, he found himself without a job in his late fifties. It was a classic story of how technology had eliminated his position—a piece of information he received in a very matter-of-fact way in 2014.

He had studied speech and communications in college and had gotten an accounting degree in his early fifties, because he was already thinking about his future. "In a way, getting laid off was a sense of relief," Paul told me. He said he pulled off to the side of the road on the way home and called his wife and three daughters to tell them that he had been laid off and wanted to take a solo trip to Florida.

When he returned from Florida, he took a part-time job driving a school bus—and he found that he actually enjoyed the work. "I've always been a shy person, and the idea of being on a bus with a bunch of kids kind of freaked me out at first," he said. But soon, he realized that after being in a dark control room for more than thirty years, it was great to be out in the sunshine, being the caretaker of the elementary school kids whom he drove. He decided to take the job full-time. What he didn't expect shortly thereafter was that his wife would ask for a divorce after more than thirty years of marriage—another loss in only a two-year period.

Then two things happened that changed his life. First, he went on a cruise by himself, and while on the ship, he encountered a solo cruises group. They brought him into their group and got him out on the dance floor, an experience that seemed to open him up in ways he had never realized. It was almost an epiphany, according to Paul: "Something happened, and I became a different person."

The second thing that changed his life happened when he got home from the cruise. He went to a wedding and watched the officiant perform the ceremony, and it occurred to him that this was something he could do and would enjoy. He did some research and learned about the Universal Life Church, an online ordination service. When he saw how easy it was to become a certified ordained minister, he signed on, and to date has performed more than 185 weddings!

As a single man in his late fifties, he had now found his own ROAR, loving his officiant work. He said it is a "10 out of 10" with regard to satisfaction. And by the way, he still drives the school bus. But his story doesn't end there. With his new love of dancing, he started going out with friends to some local clubs. In 2017, he met another dancer, one whom he loved spending time with. She is now his wife, Stacey.

When I asked him about his new life, now that he is sixty, Paul said he is thriving. He enjoys his new work, he and his wife love to travel, he's playing in a marching band and a fife-and-drum group, and of course, he's doing his fair share of dancing.

ROAR TIP

Being fired, getting divorced, failing at a business—things that people once carried as a stigma or burden—have become much less remarkable in today's world. They are just jumping-off points for reimagining who you want to be in your future. Take your losses and failures in stride and use them as your bridge to an exciting new venture.

Tom Arnott[8] is an example of someone who turned his loss into his own opportunity. A native of Toronto, at age forty he moved to the States to become senior vice president of a major commercial real estate company. When he was nearing fifty years old, the company went bankrupt. Fortunately, he found an opportunity with a real estate company, a place where he worked for three years. As he was approaching fifty-four, he made the decision to start a whole new business in developing residential homes on the East End of Long Island.

Tom called a friend who was a real estate agent, floating the idea of doing a project together. They started a building development company from scratch, working as general contractors, with no real experience. They relied on local architects to design the houses, opting for unique floor plans and being inventive with materials. By forming partnerships with local craftspeople, they were able to line up carpenters and the actual builders to complete their first project, which they sold immediately.

Over the next fifteen years, they built one high-end house a year, all within fifteen miles of each other. "If you are hyperlocal, you really get to know the market," Tom explained, as he built a profitable business and a reputation for building unique homes that always attracted an immediate buyer.

Now in his seventies, he continues to watch the marketplace for future opportunities, with an eye on producing smaller houses, as he thinks that is an emerging niche for people who don't want a big sprawling house. From the potential threat of a changing commercial real estate business, Tom took control of his own life and moved into a whole new area of real estate, a sector that had always intrigued him.

The ROAR Into survey included the following question: "Are there defining moments in your life that you would redo?" It included *yes*, *no*, and *don't know* options, and space to write in any thoughts on the subject. Seventy-six percent of people said yes, there were moments in their life they would redo. In an earlier survey question, 41 percent said if they could start their life all over again, they would.

In the written responses, the number one topic from 93 of the 312 people who wrote in was about their marriage. Many said that they would redo their marriage if they could or not be married to the person they did marry. Other responses included "I regret staying married for as long as I did" or "I got married too young and didn't have the chance to live my own life."

The second survey topic, an area commented on by 62 of the 312 respondents, was about education. They stated that they wished they had taken school more seriously for better prospects, that they would have taken a different course of study, or in some cases that they would have finished college. (To note, 52 percent of the total 630 respondents were college graduates or had one or more post-graduate degrees.)

The undertone of regret or failure in certain areas came through in many of the responses, but in the overall survey, a full 70 percent considered themselves to be happy people, and 67 percent said that there is still much more they want to achieve in their lives.

Optimism about the future is an energy force that we can join in on at any time. One of my favorite regular reads is the *Journal of Positive Psychology*, within which studies explore measurements of life satisfaction, optimism, and methods to enhance positive psychological traits. Let's just say that optimism can beget optimistic results. Countless studies have shown that when we are positive, we can attract positive results.

My maternal grandmother (whose education never went beyond the eighth grade) understood this better than anyone I knew growing up. She drilled into me that positive thinking and visualizing a positive future were the pathway to a better life. Her influence lives with me still, as I'm always the most optimistic one in any group.

There are threats all around us—the potential of technology replacing our jobs, a natural disaster displacing us, an unexpected illness, or simply feeling overwhelmed by everyday life. Working mothers can feel threatened in a more profound way, as the majority of them play the role of family caretaker in addition to working outside the family home. Over the years, I've watched—with admiration—colleagues and clients of all levels juggle their lives in ways that astonished me. I'm an effective multitasker, but most of these working moms could run circles around me.

ROAR TIP

When threats are closing in on you, stop all that you are doing, close your eyes, and breathe. Become aware of your body and your being, and think about how you have overcome adversity and problems in the past. Remember the things that you did that helped you get to the other side of it. What did you learn? How did you get there? Use those skills of resilience that you already have.

The true threat is when we think the world is closing in on us and we lose faith in our ability to manage it. That's why clichés such as "Where there's a will there's a way" are actually life lessons. In fact, pull any cliché apart, and there is an underlying truth to it.

My go-to activity when I'm feeling overwhelmed is to lace up and go for a long run. Somehow, it puts everything in perspective for me, and I find my way back. Maybe meditation or prayer helps you. Maybe painting or cooking or doing something creative brings you back to your center. Whatever practices help keep you balanced and resilient are important to cultivate—and make a priority.

> *You have to own your losses, weaknesses, failures, and threats. Doing so is liberating and lets you focus on tomorrow.*

Ultimately, like owning your numbers, you have to own your losses, weaknesses, failures, and threats. Doing so is liberating and lets you focus on tomorrow. Don't be afraid to ask for help if you are grappling with this, and remember what my grandma once said: "Anything is possible if you stay positive; visualize it and work your darnedest to make it happen."

ROAR: Chapter Takeaways

- We all put barriers in front of us, telling ourselves that we're not good at this or that. Pick one thing you have consistently told yourself that you are not good at, and decide to tackle it head-on. You might be surprised by what you discover.
- What if a perceived weakness is actually a strength? If someone tells you that you are too emotional, why must that be seen as a weakness? Put that trait to work for you in a place that values it. Know your own EQ, your emotional intelligence quotient.
- Failure, loss, or a divorce can be the jumping-off point to your next move. Take a deep breath, have faith, and start anew. This can happen at any age and any time.
- In your life so far, you've had to cope with myriad situations. Use what you learned to get to the other side of a tough period

in the past. Can you identify what helped you move beyond those times? Write down those attributes. Keep those skills handy and use them as you confront new problems.

- Optimism is one of our most cherished mind-sets. Confidence paired with a belief in a better future is the elixir that creates innumerable positive outcomes. Practice optimism every day. My moment to do so is in the morning, just before I step out of bed. First, I am grateful for another day just to be alive! Next, I spend time thinking about what positive things I can do that day. For example, how can I help someone get through a rough patch? Or if there is a negative vibe around a business problem, what can I do that day to turn it into a positive? In that morning moment, fill your head with uplifting thoughts to fuel you for the day.

PART III

Act on What's
Next for You

7

Act Courageous and Don't Look Back

Only those who will risk going too far can possibly
find out how far one can go.
—T. S. Eliot

I've made a few observations about people in the fifty-and-up category
and their teeth. First of all, as people age, they need to take care of
their teeth! It can make all the difference, especially when you smile. And
speaking of smiling, I always make it a habit to watch people of a certain
age that I pass on the street. There is nothing worse than seeing someone
from the over-fifty crowd with a scowl, hunched over, plodding along.
It sends out a signal that you are old and tired. Watch older people who
have their shoulders back, walking confidently down the street and smiling. They exude "possibilities" and are role models for everyone.

Rid yourself of the idea that now that you are a certain age, you
need to start acting like it, moving slowly, talking slowly, becoming old
in the way you dress or act. It's a self-fulfilling prophecy that will make
you old! If you are guilty of this, ask yourself: *Why am I doing that? Who
told me I had to do that?*

> *Rid yourself of the idea that now that you are a certain age, you need
> to start acting like it, moving slowly, talking slowly, becoming old in
> the way you dress or act.*

It can be a scary moment, when you make the decision that you are ready to take a step into a new life. It's normal to have self-doubts, be anxious, or worry about whether you will succeed. But legions of people have walked this road, and they have great stories about how they found the courage to do it and how they ROARed into their second half of life.

Patricia Forehand[1] was an elementary school teacher in Perry, Georgia, a small town ninety minutes south of Atlanta. A self-defined small-town girl, she had gone off to college, then returned to Perry to marry her high school sweetheart, teach, and raise her family. "I'm kind of quiet and a bit proper," she told me. "I always thought of myself as an everyday mom, yet people always told me that I was funny and made them laugh."

One day, a friend told her that she should try stand-up comedy, an idea that was completely alien to her. Her daughter pushed her too. "What's the worst that can happen, Mama, nobody laughs?" she said.

One thing led to another, and Patricia and a bunch of friends headed to Atlanta to an open-mic session at the Laughing Skull Lounge, a comedy club in the city. "It was a completely powerful feeling. I just got onstage and let loose, and people really responded." Since then, Patricia has built a new career as a comedian, appearing in at least fifty paid shows in Atlanta; Nashville; Washington, DC; and more!

"How did this happen?" I asked her.

With her Southern charm, she replied, "You can eat a whole buffet table, if you take it one bite at a time."

After that first empowering moment in Atlanta, Patricia was hooked, so she started going to other open mics. She also took classes, particularly with Lace Larrabee, an actor and comedian who helps women who are interested in comedy. To pay for classes, Patricia stopped going to the movies and buying new clothes, instead putting her resources toward her new dream. As the oldest person in the mix, Patricia said that the other comics (who were mostly in their twenties and thirties) were very accepting, rooting for her along the way.

At times, she thought, *I'm not young enough, I'm not pretty enough, I'm not brave enough, I'm not funny enough*, but she gritted her teeth and didn't look back. At fifty-eight years old, she is having the time of her life and said that her new career will lead her to where it takes her!

Patricia's talent became the basis for her reimagination. What's your special talent? Do your friends tell you that you have an eye for photography? Or that your compassion for people is extraordinary? Or that you are a whiz at numbers? How do you start turning your talent into a new chapter in your life?

McGarvey Black[2] took a circuitous route to discovering her true profession at age sixty-two, with the publication of her first novel. I should add that this was after 177 rejections from publishers (she kept a careful spreadsheet of all responses).

ROAR TIP

Learn as much as you can about what you want to do. Small steps turn into big steps that turn into leaps and bounds into a whole new world of discovery. But you've got to take that first step!

McGarvey is married, with two children, and has held many jobs in her life, including IBM sales training, advertising sales, recruiting, and digital sales and marketing. And through it all, she has been writing. "I submitted articles to my college newspaper, wrote essays and put them in a drawer, and always had ideas for a novel in my head," she said.

In her mid-forties, she was inspired to write a screenplay. Although a friend who was in the business told her that her screenplay was terrible, he still encouraged her, even bringing her into a project he was working on. They were able to raise some money to produce it, but the idea fizzled out. At that point, McGarvey owned the fact that she loved to write, and she decided it was time to become a novelist. "I didn't really know what I was doing. I read and watched videos, went to a master class with Dan Brown, and learned how to put together a plot and ultimately to write query letters to publishers," she explained.

After she wrote her first book, she put it in a drawer because it got lots of rejection letters. Then she started writing another book. At fifty-nine, she and her husband relocated to Florida, and she committed more deeply to her goal, taking seminars and writing courses, as well as networking with other writers. She became a member of Mystery Writers of America, attended their annual SleuthFest, and joined writing critique groups. Ultimately, McGarvey homed in on eight mystery and suspense publishers who would accept submissions from unknown authors, and one of them expressed interest in her book.

Her first novel, *I Never Left*, was published in May 2019; her second novel, *The First Husband*, was released in May 2020, hitting the top one hundred on Amazon US and number ten on Kindle overall on Amazon UK. A third novel, *Without Her Consent*, was released in fall of 2020, and she has two more books in the works. "It took me a long time to figure out what I was supposed to do. I have tons of ideas and hope to be writing for years to come," she said.

She hopes she will be picked up by an agent someday and that one of her novels will actually become a movie! Once she found her true calling, McGarvey never looked back. She took steps to learn how to write, how to get published, and how to build a new life for herself, one based on a longstanding interest.

ROAR TIP

Be open to doing something completely different with your life. First, you have to commit to it and be courageous in your conviction. Identifying that "something" is your breakthrough moment, whether it is a new profession, a new relationship, or a move to a place you have dreamed about.

When Michael Evans[3] was in his forties, he had been working for a presidential candidate who stepped out of the race. When it was over, he took a three-week vacation to South America.

Always a wine lover, he included Mendoza—an important wine region in Argentina—as one of his stops. Through a friend, he was introduced to Pablo Gimenez Riili, a local whose family operated a winery in the area. Pablo generously spent two days showing Michael around the area, hosting an Argentine barbecue (called an *asado*), and of course enjoying lots of wine.

Becoming infatuated with the area, Michael thought he might buy a little piece of land and have Pablo plant some vines for him, so that Michael could become a winemaker. As he told friends back in the States, at least ten people came forward and said that they would like to do that, too! "Maybe there's a business idea here," he recalls thinking. "I could stay here for a while and put this together." He admitted that he was flying by the seat of his pants, acknowledging that not really knowing anything was a blessing in disguise.

In 2007, he and his new business partner, Pablo, along with another Argentine winemaker, planted forty acres of vines. Michael put $85,000 on his credit cards and had some friends and family members help in the original investment. Today, The Vines of Mendoza comprises 1500 acres and counts 240 wine lovers who have one to twenty acres to grow their own wines, as part of the overall effort. There is an internationally recognized resort on the property, a restaurant from Francis Mallmann (one of the premier chefs in South America), and a winemaker's village for tastings from micro-wineries.

Michael acknowledged that there have been ups and downs along the way. He adds that a business like this one—particularly in a country such as Argentina, which has its own economic fluctuations—is not for the faint of heart. "It's been hard, and if I had known how hard it would be, I might have thought again, but I do love it," he said with a laugh.

Now in its second decade of existence, The Vines of Mendoza is looking at recreating the model in other countries around the world. Fifteen years after sharing a glass of wine with someone he'd just met, Michael is still in Argentina.

Different things set different people on their journey. For Patricia, it was thinking about how she might channel her sense of humor. McGarvey knew she had always loved writing; she just needed to hone her skill and mold it into publishable form. As for Michael, a moment of serendipity spun out into a major life development.

Being courageous in stepping out can also be brought about by an unexpected illness or the realization that your kids are all grown up and the world is yours to take. Or maybe a gnawing feeling that you should be doing something with your innate talents nudges you into action.

Debra Shriver[4] has always had a curiosity about the world, and it led to an amazing journey. From a small Alabama town ninety minutes from Mobile, at eighteen she headed to the University of Alabama. There she earned a master's in journalism, paid for by jobs and student loans. "I was the first child and the only girl, and I grew up in the civil rights era, where I saw a lot of changes around me. I wanted to learn more, so I read lots of books and knew there was a big world out there," she said, reminiscing about her youth. Upon graduation, she moved to Pensacola, Florida, where she worked for a small ad agency and then the local newspaper, where she met her future husband.

The couple later moved to Washington, DC, where Debra became one of the youngest vice presidents at a major advertising agency before moving on to other important roles in marketing and communications in the area. Ultimately, she was recruited for a major communications–public relations job in New York City, and she made the leap. There she excelled for years, establishing herself as one of the top communications officers in the city. Life was pretty amazing for someone who had come from that small town in Alabama. Her days were filled with exciting work, and she and her husband enjoyed all that the New York cultural and food scene had to offer.

In her mid-fifties, Debra learned that she was in the early stages of Parkinson's disease, and it made her stop to take a hard look at her future. "For two years, I knew something was wrong, but I didn't know what it was," she said. "I ate right and exercised, but it wasn't until a European doctor diagnosed it that it became a reality."

While she continued to work, at one point, Debra decided that she needed a break. "I looked around me. There weren't many women in the executive suite, and people my age were starting to have heart attacks. I was working harder than ever, and I knew I had to do something. I had always been a Francophile, which is why my husband and I bought a house in New Orleans, a city that has a strong French influence. But now I wanted to do what many people call the 'French leave.'"

She took a leave of absence, and for the next eight and a half months she lived in Paris, with an occasional trip back to the States. "I learned how not to have a real schedule. I took lots of classes in cooking and photography and calligraphy, but I just liked sitting in the cafés and watching people. I was fortunate to be able to have this experience," she acknowledged.

Ultimately, Debra decided not to go back to work, stepping out at the peak of her experience, and she moved to New Orleans full-time. Once she was there, she sold the house, found an apartment, got divorced, and as she put it, "Stepped into the process of becoming newly single for the first time in thirty-eight years!"

Debra has started her own company, which centers on house renovations. She also sells her photography to designers and is launching a small book imprint. "I'm hatching plans that I've dreamed about for years, things that I rediscovered as I went back to read through the thirty journals that I've kept over my life. I see myself as someone who has never been risk averse. Once I decide on something, I never look back. I believe in my own world and what I can create," she explained.

When I asked her how she wanted to be remembered someday, she replied, "I want people to say that she was involved, present, engaged." Debra is one of the courageous ones who will always forge a future path.

Pamela[5] is yet another fearless person I spoke to, one I'd call a "serial reimagineer." Sixty years old, single, and an empty nester, she picked up her life and moved to Los Angeles for a job. And it wasn't her first reimagining. Earlier, as a working mom who had taken on a master's degree in business, she had climbed the ranks in the beauty industry, becoming one of the most senior brand leaders in the category.

When she was in her mid-forties, Pamela had begun to question the path she was on. "I wondered if selling another lipstick was really what I wanted," she said. "Isn't there something else?" That set her on a path of discovery, first by expanding her role into the area of corporate reputation, particularly in the environment and social justice areas. As she learned more about sustainability, she realized that she had a passion for it.

At fifty, Pamela enrolled in a master's program to study the science of sustainability. One of her kids was in college and the other two were still in high school, so she joined them as a fellow student. "There's always a way to do it, especially if you can get financial assistance from your company," she explained. She filled in with her own savings, and even though she was the oldest person in the class, she reveled in the knowledge she was gaining. She finished the program in two years.

From there, she took her first pivot into the sustainability practice of one of the top global beauty companies. Once all of her kids were in college, she moved from the suburbs into the city. On the personal front, Pamela tried online dating, but she didn't find anyone for her. "I think the universe makes it happen for you when you are ready," she said. She met David on a train platform and Jon in the elevator of her apartment building, but those dates didn't lead to anything serious. "I'm at the stage in my life where I can be happy alone with the company of good friends and family. I don't really need a man to feel complete," she explained.

As she approached her sixtieth birthday, she got a call from a major global company in Los Angeles to head up their sustainability practice. "When they asked me my age, I hesitated, but then I put it right out there."

Leaving her kids on the East Coast and a two-year love interest behind, Pamela packed her bags and moved west. She's not sure what will become of her beau, but she said that she can't worry about it now, because at this amazing time in her life, the adventure is all about her. She hopes her new job will give her a terrific ten-year run, and from there, she already knows she wants to teach, consult, and keep up on all things sustainable.

Pamela started her journey in her mid-forties, putting in the time to think about her life, especially when her kids were out of the nest. To her friends and colleagues, she has become a role model for doing it right, step by step until she fully ROARed into her sixties.

The stories in this chapter underscore that it takes courage to step into the unknown. Patricia didn't even know what stand-up comedy meant, but she took the leap. In his wildest dreams, Michael never thought he'd be running a major vineyard in Argentina. Deb's "French leave" led to a life of rediscovering long-dreamed-of plans. And Pamela showed us that it is possible to reimagine oneself over and over. Each of these brave individuals took a thread of an idea and wove a new future for themselves.

It is often said that the first step is always the hardest, yet it is also said that not taking that step may make your life harder.

It is often said that the first step is always the hardest, yet it is also said that not taking that step may make your life harder. You know that you have your dreams, and you know that you have your ideal self, as they keep recurring in your mind. Listen to the voice that beckons you, as it is your inner self telling you what is true and real in your desires.

ROAR: Chapter Takeaways

- Courage takes many forms, and it is the courageous ones who show us that all things are possible. Recall an act of courage in your own life. What was the circumstance? What did you do? How did it make you feel? Let your act of courage inspire you!

- If you had a serious health diagnosis, how would you change your life? What would you do differently with the time you have? Write it down. Now that you know what you want, why wait for that diagnosis?

- Make a decision to start something brand new. A new business, a new relationship, a new city to live in, a new workshop or class, a new hobby—these are all moves that will set you on a path to discovery.

- Never lose sight of your vision for yourself. You may have twists and turns, but if you stay devoted to your goal to write that book or build that new company—you will do it. Obstacles are a natural part of life, and they can be overcome! Step around them and through them. Better yet, jump over them.

8

Act Now with Life Layering

We don't grow older, we grow riper.
—Pablo Picasso

You don't have to quit your job or abandon your career to try something new. All you need to do is *add another layer* to your life. I started doing this when I was in my late thirties. I had decided I was the most boring person I knew, and I vowed to change that. I couldn't quit my job—and I didn't want to, because I enjoyed what I was doing—so I investigated how I could *add* to my life.

> *You don't have to quit your job or abandon your career to try something new. All you need to do is* add another layer *to your life.*

I had worked hard since coming to New York at twenty-one with only $60 in my pocket. I was a reporter for a daily menswear publication and then switched to the advertising side of the business. I climbed the ladder and became publisher of *GQ* magazine at thirty-four years old (the youngest publisher in the national magazine industry at the time). *GQ* was a great place to work; I loved what I was doing. I thought it was one of the best jobs in the world, and it came with terrific perks. I met the celebrities who appeared on the covers of the magazine, including Cary Grant and Michael Jordan. I had dinner at Giorgio Armani's house and did business with so many amazing people. I led sales meetings in the Caribbean and traveled to Paris and Milan on a regular basis, as well as mentored people who became stars in the magazine industry.

But I was working harder than ever. In fact, it seemed that all I was doing was working. I traveled 40 percent of the time—I was away from home almost two weeks out of every month on business trips. I spent most weekends going to trade shows and conferences. The European menswear shows were held during the Fourth of July and Labor Day weekends (American holidays not observed in Europe), so I often missed out on those celebrations with family and friends. My life then might sound glamorous, but the reality was harsher than people usually realize. Yes, it's nice to be doing business in Italy, but at the end of the day, it was still hard work and long days.

That's where I found myself on a Fourth of July weekend in Florence. It was ten o'clock at night, and I had finally sat down to eat dinner in my hotel room after an endless day of meetings with advertisers. Although my room had a lovely view of the city and its magnificent Arno River, I was too exhausted to even appreciate it. This was the third year in a row that I had spent this holiday weekend working, away from the beach party I knew was going on back home, where all my friends were. I wanted to be there with them, not in Italy eating alone.

My thirty-ninth birthday was coming up, and I had been thinking a lot about my life and how I was spending my time. Approaching forty is a milestone for most people, and for the previous year, I had had a nagging feeling that I was missing out on something, in spite of my terrific job. I had been pushing such thoughts away, but they kept resurfacing. When I stepped back from the day-to-day hustle of running the business side of the magazine—meetings, meetings, and more meetings— I realized that all I was doing was working. I didn't have much of a social life, and although I had a lot of friends and was close to my family, I didn't get to spend enough time with them.

That's when I decided I needed to change the direction my life was taking, or it would become completely one-dimensional. I would be a successful magazine executive, but that's all I would be. And although that might seem like enough to some people, it wasn't enough for me. I wanted to do *more* with my life. I wanted a multidimensional life that was not defined by my work.

Like most people, I wasn't in a position to simply quit my job. Few people are wealthy enough to stop working—and even those who are don't want to do nothing all day! I knew I needed to find a way to reimagine my life to include my job and work while expanding to accommodate even more. That's when I came up with this idea I called "life layering." I was determined to add another layer to my life, on top of the job I had worked hard to get and enjoyed doing.

On the flight home from Italy, I thought further about what I might explore. I've always had a strong adventurous streak, so my preliminary list included quite a few extreme activities. I considered going helicopter skiing or race-car driving. Getting a motorcycle license and buying a Harley. Learning to sail on the Long Island Sound. Learning to fly— a fantasy ever since being a kid obsessed with planes. Going on safari in Africa and climbing Mt. Kilimanjaro—a dream inspired by reading Ernest Hemingway's "The Snows of Kilimanjaro" in eleventh-grade English class. By the time I landed at Kennedy Airport, I had narrowed the list to three adventures I was determined to try: driving a race car, learning to fly, and going to Africa.

ROAR TIP

Start your own life-layering project. Grab a journal or a notebook and write your goals for the coming year, in all aspects of your life—work, hobbies and leisure activities, personal relationships, and so on. (I'm not the first person to say this, but I truly believe that the very act of *writing them* is a critical factor in achieving those goals, because now you have something tangible to refer to.) The next step is to review this list of goals at least once a month throughout the year, to remind you of what you set out to achieve and to gauge how much progress you have—or haven't!—made. Writing the list and putting it away won't do you any good: *you need to keep checking on yourself.*

As mentioned, I narrowed my list to three activities that most appealed to me. The first one I tried was race-car driving, but it didn't live up to my expectations. I tested the waters by taking some of my clients out for a day at the Skip Barber Racing School in Lakeville,

Connecticut, and we all had a great time. It was a lot of fun, and I learned a few things—about how to lean into a curve, for instance. Overall, though, going around and around in circles didn't hold my interest or satisfy my thirst for adventure. Still, it was a valuable experience because it showed me one thing I *didn't* want to pursue. And I was able to find that out through my work, while entertaining clients.

If you can try exploring activities you think you might be interested in through your own work, by all means do so. Maybe your company will pay for you to take an evening class in some subject related to your work. If you love it, wonderful: you've found something you want to learn about even more. If you don't, you've taken only one course, which probably lasted only a couple of months. Or maybe your job has after-work activities you can explore, such as a softball league or expert talks on a subject that interests you. Maybe your company supports a volunteer day—as many companies do—and you can see what types of charity efforts appeal to you. And if your work involves entertaining clients (as mine did), consider other events or activities that might interest you as well as them.

> **ROAR TIP**
>
> Before you commit to becoming an expert in something, try it out. There's no sense diving into something until you're sure you're going to enjoy it. Do a test run or two and make sure it meets or exceeds your expectations.

Once you've determined what it is you want to become an expert on, make a lifetime commitment to it. Do you want to be a nutrition expert? A pro photographer? Accomplished in fine woodworking? A master in some competitive sport? An opera buff? Your goals will be different from mine and other people's, but whatever they are, *commit* to them. Then think about what you want to *do* with that expertise. Do you want to give seminars or TED Talks? Do you want to teach? Do you want to write about what you've learned and what you know? Or simply be known in your circle and community as the go-to person on that subject? Whatever your goal is, own that commitment.

If you're having a tough time figuring out what you want to try, think about what excited you when you were younger. When you were a kid, what wild things did you want to do? No matter how unusual they were, maybe you can pursue one of those dreams now. Perhaps you enjoyed baking cookies with your mom and dreamed of becoming a pastry chef. Just because you didn't pursue that as a profession doesn't mean you can't take a course and start whipping up fabulous desserts again or even launching a new business. Maybe you wanted to be a rock star. If you're in mid-career or post-career, it's probably too late for you to pursue that full-time. (Sorry to break it to you!) But it's not too late to form a band with friends, neighbors, or coworkers. You don't have to be world-famous to enjoy jamming in your spare time. Then again, you might become a famous rocker in your fifties!

Maybe you wanted to write book reviews for the *New York Times*. That's a tough job to get, but you can indulge your inner critic by joining—or starting—a book club. In my case, I've long been fascinated with planes. I don't remember when this obsession started, but I know I was younger than ten when I used to ask my parents to drive past the airport where we lived in Pittsburgh so I could see the planes taking off and landing. I joined the Civil Air Patrol, an organization affiliated with the US Air Force, because they were supposed to teach young people to fly. I flirted with the idea of joining the Air Force. I considered becoming a professional pilot. Although I didn't do either of those things, the desire to fly stayed with me.

So, as my fortieth birthday approached and I was thinking about adding another layer to my life, I considered anew the idea of learning to fly. I thought, *If not now, when?* The very next weekend, I drove to the nearest regional airport and asked, "Where can I take a flying lesson?" The woman behind the counter said she could sign me up, and I had my first lesson the next weekend. An instructor and I took off, and as soon as we were out over the Atlantic Ocean, the pilot stalled the plane. I think that was his way of testing me, to see how serious I was about wanting to fly. If I had been afraid, he would have discouraged me from pursuing this. But I was absolutely exhilarated. I went back the next weekend for my second lesson. I was hooked. I knew flying was for me and made the commitment to get my pilot's license.

People have often asked me when I had time to take flying lessons. Yes, I was busy at work, but I didn't work *all* the time. I did travel for my job, and there were times when I was away over a weekend, so I couldn't take lessons every weekend, but I scheduled them whenever I could. I made flying a priority in my life. We all have the same number of hours in a day, a week, a month, a year; the difference is in how we spend that time. I needed to have sixty hours of flight time before I could take my exams and get my license. I didn't rush it; I didn't set a self-imposed deadline, because I wanted to learn the right way. I took lessons over the next two to three years, learning everything I needed to know to fly safely.

After I got my license, I flew regularly for the next twenty years. I loved flying; it was a counterbalance to my office job in publishing. It even added a new dimension to my personality, because it forced me to be calm in all situations. You can't panic when something unusual happens while you're flying; you need to figure out what's wrong, request help if you need it, and land safely.

Finally, if you had the same childhood dream that I did and want to pursue flying but wonder if you can afford it, check out the University Aviation Association at uaa.aero for a listing of over seven hundred aviation scholarships available to people of any age.

ROAR TIP

The key point is, if you want to expand through life layering, you need to make your new interest a top priority. Commit to it. Make time for it. And that might require giving up something else. You can't do everything—nobody can—so go after what's deeply important to you. When you do, you'll reap the rewards. Adding a new layer of expertise or experience to your life is incredibly satisfying.

Tom DeVincentis[1] is a veterinarian who had a well-known practice in New York City called The Country Vet. When you stepped into his place, you thought you were in a small town in Ohio. He even wrote a book called *Tails of the City*, a charming collection of short stories about

being a Manhattan pet veterinarian. While it was a small-animal practice, his desire to become a veterinarian was rooted in hanging around
the racetrack as a kid in Ohio, where his dad owned a horse. Horses
were his first love. In his late fifties he decided to get back to his early
dreams about horses. Local riding lessons led to joining a fox hunt club
(they don't hunt actual foxes anymore), which earned him ribbons and
his "pinks," the scarlet-colored jackets proudly worn by those with supe-
rior horsemanship. He learned jumping and competed in local horse
shows. Ultimately he bought his own horse, Polly, and now in his early
seventies, he continues to ride regularly. Tom added a layer to his life
that continues to thrill him.

The other activity I pursued as part of my "adventure layer" was
traveling the world. I caught the travel bug early: I took my first plane
ride when I was ten years old. As mentioned, I was obsessed with
planes, so after a while, it wasn't enough for me to *watch* the planes
taking off; I wanted to fly in one. I begged my parents, and they found
a way to make it happen. My father's brother and his wife lived in New
York City, so I was to fly there and visit them for a week. My parents
didn't have the money for the whole family to go, so they arranged
for me to fly—alone. My mother took me onto the plane—which
you could still do back then—and she handed me into the care of a
flight attendant. When the plane took off, I felt like I was in a rocket
ship. My ten-year-old self thought, *This is my destiny; this is what I'm
supposed to be doing!*

I wanted to fly again as soon as I could. And I did, just a few
years later. My uncle and aunt had gone to Ireland to trace some of
our ancestors, and as soon as I heard about their trip, I decided that I
wanted to go to Ireland, too. The fact that I was only twelve didn't faze
me in the least.

When I asked my parents if I could go, they said, "If you can save
up the money, you can go." I'm guessing they thought it would never
happen, so that was an easy way for them to avoid having to say no. But
I was determined, and I did everything a twelve-year-old kid can do to
earn money over the next year. I shoveled snow for all the neighbors.
I mowed lawns. I delivered newspapers. And by the next summer, I
had saved more than $300, which was enough for a round-trip flight

to Ireland at the time. When I showed my parents how much I had in my bank account, they knew they needed to honor their promise, and again, they made it happen.

And again, I flew alone.

My parents put me on a plane in Pittsburgh; I flew to New York, where my uncle met me and made sure I got on the right flight; then I flew to Shannon, Ireland, where my cousin Vera met me. When I tell people this story, they often ask me if my parents were crazy or if I was just exceptionally mature, because crossing the ocean in those days was like flying to the moon. It was exotic and hard to imagine. My parents got some pushback for sending me alone, but they didn't have the money to go with me, and they arranged for me to always be with a family member, except while on the flight itself. Their support of me was a great gift, and I appreciate it to this day. Of course, kids today much more commonly travel unaccompanied, so I guess I was just ahead of my time! And although I was just an ordinary thirteen-year-old and not very worldly, I was ambitious, and I was determined to bust out of the life I had in Pittsburgh.

I remember being on the plane, thinking, *I have no idea where I'm going or what the next few weeks will be like*, but it didn't matter to me. I was off to see the world! I was a little shy when I met Vera, but she was warm and welcoming, and she made me feel comfortable right away. During the next few weeks, Vera and her family drove me all over Ireland, showing me as much of their glorious country as we had time for. Before I returned to the States, my parents had arranged for me to stay abroad for another week to visit my grandmother's sister in England and see some of London. It was an amazing adventure, and when I got home, I remember telling my parents, "I'm going to spend the rest of my life traveling the world."

I was pretty happy with my travel at that point: my first plane ride at ten, my first international flight at thirteen. Then, when I was a freshman in college, some of my older classmates told me they had been backpacking in Europe over the summer. I was immediately interested. I thought the kids who went must be rich, but they told me they flew to Amsterdam, round trip on Dutch airline KLM, for only $200. That was cheap! I was determined to do it.

Of course, I would need money to live and travel while I was there, and I didn't have any. I worked all four years of college just to pay for my tuition and expenses. But I was dead set on going, so I used some of my college-loan money to fund my trip. That meant I had to take out another student loan to pay off the first one, but that was a trade-off I was willing to make. So, on May 1, as soon as my classes for the semester ended, I flew to Amsterdam. I had arranged to join a mini-tour with a group, at first: we traveled to Denmark, Sweden, Finland, and on to the Soviet Union. Then I left the group, got a Eurail Pass, and made my way west to as many countries on the continent as possible: Poland, Germany, Belgium, Luxembourg, France, Switzerland, Italy, Austria, and Spain. I backpacked around for four months, until the day before classes started up again in the fall. I had the adventure of my life! I was just a working-class kid, and I remember thinking, *I hope I can do this again someday*.

Over the next few years or so, I didn't get to travel that much. We all know how the early days of working full-time—whether it's just a job or you're building a career—become consumed with paying your rent and other bills and dealing with the day-to-day chores and errands of everyday life. Still, I took whatever time I could and went to Mexico, the Caribbean, California—wherever I could afford to go. It wasn't until I was in my thirties and I started traveling on business that I was able to significantly feed my travel bug again. I went to Europe four times a year for trade shows, and I tacked on an extra day or two whenever possible. It allowed me to ski in Austria, hike in the Alps, and explore Corsica. And it was during that trip to Italy, before my fortieth birthday, that I decided I wanted to see the world in a more adventurous way.

I called my closest friends and invited them to come with me and climb Mt. Kilimanjaro in Tanzania, to fulfill that childhood dream I mentioned earlier in this book. Seven of us went, and it was a magnificent experience. To add to the adventure, I set it up as a fundraiser for the Starlight Children's Foundation, an organization I was involved in, raising several thousand dollars to help seriously ill kids make their dreams come true. Ultimately, I would add a fundraiser to other adventures to Nepal and Patagonia, a great way to share my experiences with people who supported me.

Starting at forty, I also decided that I would take all the vacation time and personal days that my company gave me. Many people don't do this; they think they're "heroes" for working so hard and *not* taking their vacation time. Some believe they're too busy (or too important) to be away from work. But the business will continue to run when you're not there. We all need to step away from time to time, get some perspective, refresh and recharge, have some downtime. All of that makes us *better*, not worse, at our jobs and in our work. You're entitled to vacation and personal days, and you should take them. Whenever I would get a new boss, I would make sure it was clear that those free days were important to me.

> **ROAR TIP**
>
> Take time off—and use your vacation time as an opportunity to have an adventure, to explore, and to renew yourself.

That doesn't mean you have to go gallivanting all over the world. That was what *I* wanted to do. You can take a staycation, if that's your pleasure. You can go to a beach, a lake, a park, or your backyard. You can visit your parents, family, friends—whether they're across town, across the state, or across the country. You can spend time on your art, your music, your language, or whatever creative talent you have or want to develop. The key is to put effort into that "layer" during your free time.

When I was in my early forties, I heard about an organization called the Travelers' Century Club, for people who have been to at least one hundred countries. I thought, *That sounds like a fun goal*, and I immediately aimed for increasing my travels even more so I could join. It was really just a badge of honor, that members are well-traveled individuals, but I wanted that badge! Fortunately, my family and friends indulge me in my quest to run around the world, oftentimes giving up holidays with me. In my fiftieth year, I reached that goal, when I went to Antarctica with a group of friends: it was my hundredth country and my seventh continent. I have a photo of me and my friends unfurling a banner with the message, "Antarctica, 100 countries!" That was the capstone of my globe-trotting and travel years. I still travel extensively: in

2020, just before the pandemic, I visited my 124th country (Ethiopia), and I plan to keep exploring as long as I can.

In my early fifties, something presented itself that also became a new layer for me. My sister Peg called and asked if I would run a marathon with her. I hadn't run the 26.2-mile race in over twenty-five years, opting for 10ks and the occasional half marathon, but something sparked inside that maybe I had one more marathon in me. We decided on the London marathon, as it was taking place during her birthday week, and we made the plan for a year out. The night before the race, we went to a *Runner's World* party and met a man who had run all seven continents, and I thought, *Now that is a cool idea*.

Flash-forward: it became my new mini-layer. Deciding to run one marathon a year, Peg and I went to Buenos Aires, the Gold Coast of Australia, Tanzania, Toronto, and Mongolia to run six of the continents together and I went on to run Antarctica (to celebrate my sixtieth birthday), becoming one of fewer than one thousand people in the world to have run seven marathons on seven continents. A serendipitous moment at a running party sparked a whole new layering idea for me and reintroduced me to long-distance running. I continue to run a marathon every year and will do so for as long as I am able.

ROAR TIP

People ask me how I manage to get in so much travel. The answer lies in precision planning and setting a schedule a year in advance. It also includes side excursions on business trips and tacking on a day or two to long holiday weekends (yes, a five-day trip to a city like Budapest is a great way to spend Thanksgiving weekend). Thanks to the airline industry and plenty of frequent-flier miles, a lot of my flight costs are covered. My other trick is to keep a separate travel bank account. It can only be touched for travel, and I budget it accordingly. As travel is a personal priority, I always manage to put some extra cash into that account.

Once you have a layer fully integrated into your life, it's time to add something else. I'm big on milestone birthdays, so I've added something every ten years. But as I approached my fiftieth birthday, I wanted to stretch even further. If my forties were my "adventure" years, I decided my fifties would be my "creative" years. I had been interested in photography since my first trip to Ireland. I had taken my father's Argus camera (this was years before cell phone cameras) so I would have pictures to remind me of all the wonderful things I saw in the country of my ancestors. When I backpacked in Europe the summer after my freshman year in college, I took hundreds of pictures—again, because I thought this was a once-in-a-lifetime trip that I would not be able to replicate. I thought I would never have another opportunity to travel to so many places and see so many wonderful sights.

Much later, when my friends and I decided to go to Antarctica, I bought my first digital camera, a Nikon D2. I actually took both a film camera and the digital camera on the trip, but when I took note of how fast I could view and work with my digital pictures, I never went back to film. The precision of digital photography, the immediacy of reviewing my work, and the efficiency of the entire process appealed to my time-management obsession.

Since I enjoyed taking pictures (and still do!), I decided to learn as much as I could about the art of photography. In the evenings after work, I took courses at two New York institutions, the School of Visual Arts and the International Center of Photography (ICP). I studied the work of a vast range of photographers: Ansel Adams, Robert Capa, Helmut Newton, Walker Evans, Weegee, and more. I read photography books about these photographers and about the technical and artistic aspects of creating an excellent picture. I went to photography auctions at Sotheby's and Christie's; photography galleries in lower Manhattan; exhibits at the ICP in midtown (where I eventually joined the acquisitions committee and later the board); and the world's largest international art fair devoted to photography, sponsored by the Association of International Photography Art Dealers (AIPAD). I taught myself Photoshop and other technical aspects of altering my pictures.

In other words, I jumped into the deep end, headfirst, immersing myself to learn as much as I could. All that learning influenced my eye, my technique, and my skill to help me become a better photographer. And my efforts paid off: I often showed photographs from my travels to friends (don't we all?), and one of my friends was an artist who noticed how much improved my photos had become over time. She said, "You have some really amazing photos. You should cull the best of your work and display them, in a show."

At first, I said, "That's a crazy idea. I'm not a great photographer, I just have a few great photographs." I wasn't a professional photographer, and I had no intention of trying to become one. But I realized that if I could sell some of my work, that would be a great way to raise funds for one of my favorite charities, the Starlight Children's Foundation.

I agreed to exhibit my photography and held what today would be considered a pop-up show. Over the next few weeks, after work, I reviewed the thousands of pictures I had taken over the years, selecting and reselecting to narrow the field until I had about two hundred I thought were my best. About 150 people came to the show, and I sold over one hundred photos. That led to another show, at The Explorers Club in Manhattan, which led to other shows in New Orleans and Chicago. In the long run, photography not only satisfied my creative interests but also created a fulfilling layer in my life.

You don't have to be interested in photography—that's not the point. But we all have a creative gene, whether you doodle and draw funny cartoons, knit or crochet or sew, paint or sculpt, bake scrumptious desserts, sing or dance or play an instrument, or write mysteries or science fiction novels in your spare time. We all have *some* creative ability; you simply need to find yours and then *mine* it.

> *We all have* some *creative ability; you simply need to find yours and then* mine *it.*

Don't worry about what other people think: you have to accept that not everyone will like what you do. Some will say, "You're just an amateur." Others will say, "You really have talent!" Whatever it is, it only matters that you are happy doing something creative, which adds value to your life. As the old saying goes, "Nothing ventured, nothing gained."

And don't make excuses. Avoid saying, "I don't have time." We all have the same amount of time; it's how we spend it that differs. If you have one evening a week free, you can take a course. If you have an hour a day free (at lunch, during your commute, or before you go to sleep), you can read a book that will teach you more about the creative craft you want to pursue. Yes, you'll need to replace something else in your day. Maybe you won't be able to follow the news as thoroughly as you used to. Maybe you'll have to watch less television or stop binge-watching a show on Netflix. Maybe you can't have as many lunches with friends. Maybe you'll have to find ways to multitask, so you can do laundry and work on a project simultaneously. But if you really want to find the time for your new life layer, you can.

ROAR TIP

One of the best things about adding new layers to your life and expanding your interests is that they often lead to something you might never have considered doing otherwise.

At one of my photography shows, my friend Jaqui Lividini told me how much she liked my work, and said, "Why don't you do a book of your photography? If you do, we'll launch it at Saks." At the time, Jaqui was head of fashion merchandising and communications for Saks Fifth Avenue. I said I'd think about it, but truth to tell, I didn't give it a second thought until I ran into her again a few weeks later, and she asked me if I was working on the book.

I confessed that I wasn't, because I honestly didn't know where to begin. She said she would connect me with someone she knew. And a week later, I had lunch with Jaqui's friend Marta Hallett, who had her own imprint at Glitterati, which publishes singular illustrated books. As I told Marta about my travels to a hundred countries, she recognized how unusual an achievement that is and said, "I want to do a book with you." I said I didn't even know what the book would be, and she said we would figure that out together. That lunch led to the publication of my first book, *Wanderlust: 100 Countries, A Personal Journey.* As promised, Saks launched it. The *New York Times* featured it in its holiday book guide; *American Photo* magazine named it one of the best photography books of the year; and it became a bestseller in its genre.

None of that would have happened if I hadn't been open to the ideas of my well-meaning friends. So, I decided my fifties would be my creative years. Over the next ten years or so, Glitterati published more collections of my photography, which has been such a rewarding creative outlet for me.

My life layer of adventure travel also led to another creative outlet: I started writing again, which I hadn't done since my first job out of college, at Fairchild Publications. As mentioned, I like milestones, so as the year 2000 approached, I wanted to do something special to celebrate the new century. I planned a trip with an exotic element to it: I decided to go to Namibia and South Africa with some friends. Our group arranged to have a plane for a week with a South African pilot, and I also made arrangements to pilot the plane myself. Namibia is a spectacular place to take photos, and I captured breathtaking moments with my camera.

When I came home, I was very excited about the trip, and I was very proud of the pictures I had taken. When I showed them to my friend Pamela Fiori, the editor-in-chief of *Town & Country*, she asked me to write a story about my trip to Namibia. I hadn't written professionally in twenty-five years, but she encouraged me to take a crack at it, and the magazine published it. That reignited my interest in writing, and I realized how much I had missed it. And that added yet another creative layer to my life. I commenced writing travel pieces for a variety of publications, such as the *New York Times* and travel media brands such as AFAR. I should mention that Hearst published *Town & Country* at the time, but with many of the other outlets, I had no connections. I pitched stories, got rejections, and had some hits. But most of all I was persistent.

We all have talents, skills, hobbies, and interests we've left behind along the way to adulthood. Maybe you played soccer or baseball as a kid but gave it up when it became clear that you weren't going to be a professional sports hero. Maybe you played in your high school marching band or jazz band but gave that up when you realized it wasn't your destiny to be a musician full-time. Think of all the activities you pursued when you were a kid—and all you left behind when you "grew up" and spent most of your time at work. Now is the time to resurrect or enhance them.

Andrew Carter[2] has spent his whole professional career as a sales executive in the leather goods business. Years ago, however, he added a life layer by becoming a judge in the dog world. As a breeder and judge of Corgis, he has traveled the world, from the UK to Russia to South Africa, to judge at nearly fifty dog shows, including Crufts in England and Westminster in New York. He's known around the world as a leading Corgi expert, as well as a go-to person for those who want to bring a dog into their life. In fact, he's so accomplished with all things canine that he has entered the industry as the COO of a new company called K9 Wear that manufactures and sells dog apparel and harnesses. His life layer has now become his business.

> **ROAR TIP**
>
> No matter how many hours you work, you still have time to indulge a passion. If you can get up early and do something you love before work, do that. Many people start their day by running, cycling, or working out either at home, at the gym, or outdoors. That's a great way to enjoy whatever physical activity appeals to you, while at the same time getting your blood flowing so you're ready to face the workday and whatever it brings.

Other people wake early to paint or write. My friend Kate White was editor in chief of *Cosmopolitan* magazine and mother of two children. When she decided to add another layer to her life, she woke up every day at 5 AM to work on her writing career. That was fifteen years ago, and since then, she has left her job at the magazine and embraced writing full-time. And she has published thirteen suspense novels, including *Such a Perfect Wife*.

If you're not an early riser, try to find time after work to devote to your passion. I'm not a morning person, and I needed to be at the office by 7:30 or 8, so getting up at 5 AM to write or work on my photography just wasn't going to happen. So, I pursued all my creative activities after work, cramming in as much as I could in the evenings. Instead of viewing my after-work hours as simply time to eat, decompress, chill out, and go to sleep, I planned every evening I could so it would be as productive as possible.

That's not as daunting as it sounds. One of my role models is Teddy Roosevelt, who valued the importance of living "a strenuous life"—which he clearly did, considering all he accomplished. Winston Churchill is another role model, for the same reason: not only a political giant, he won the Nobel Prize in Literature and was an accomplished and prolific amateur painter of landscapes and portraits. I realize I'll never achieve what those great men did, but that doesn't mean I can't strive to be as accomplished and productive as possible in my life, doing things that matter to me. I was a multitasker before it was even a word; I've always had five things going at one time. And I should add that while I was building all of my layers, I continued to grow in my professional life, climbing the executive ranks until becoming the president and publishing director of Hearst.

ROAR TIP

Start planning your weekends so they don't get sucked up in chores and errands. Find a way to knock those out during the week, so you can, for example, take flying lessons on weekends, as I did. I regularly check my calendar to see when and where I have free time, and then I'm planning that time so I can spend it on projects that are important to me. I've honed that skill over many years, but even if you haven't yet, you can start now.

Don't waste time; every day of your life should be meaningful. That requires structuring how you live your life to maximize how much you can accomplish in any given day, week, and month. And that means every hour too. In my case, I rejected everything extraneous to my goals. I've never wanted to sit on the sofa and watch a ball game or hang out at a bar for four hours. My friends know I don't do lunch or brunch because that sucks a huge number of precious hours out of the middle of a day. Don't get me wrong: It's important to have time to relax and renew yourself, and I do when I go for my daily run or when I'm reading a good book. It's important to have a social life, and I see my family and friends for dinner or a drink, though it's more likely we'll be doing something together, rather than just hanging out. I continually strive toward a more productive life.

Maximize your time so you can do the things you really want to do. When your kids reach a certain age, they can be more independent. Set the ground rules early that you have your own personal priorities. Finally, you don't need to give up sleep to do this. Many people think the only way to get more done is to sleep less. I sleep seven hours a night. To do that, I make every waking moment count.

Make every waking moment count.

I continue to add new layers to my life. I still enjoy my adventure layer—traveling to new places as well as favorites—and I always have a camera with me, continuing to improve my craft while finding satisfaction through my photography layer. I added a philanthropy layer for my sixties. Some friends and I started a foundation, and I have enrolled in a master's program at Columbia University to learn all I can about non-profit management—which I'll tell more about in chapter 12, "Reassess Your Community and Your Relationship with It." That is my next layer. I'm excited to see what I'll pursue in the years ahead, and I hope my experiences and suggestions inspire you to add layers to your life, too.

ROAR: Chapter Takeaways

- When you have your *aha* moment that it is time for a change, you can't ignore it, as it will follow you and remind you—and then hound you. That means it is decision time.
- Life layering is a concept that lets you build new levels of knowledge and expertise into your life. One of mine was to become a global adventure traveler, and I've spent twenty-five years pursuing that goal. Aside from enriching my own life, it has allowed me to be the de facto travel consultant for friends and colleagues! Keep adding layers in other areas, once you have built a foundation with earlier ones.
- Once upon a time, if you didn't take your vacation, it was a badge of honor. But everyone needs to rest and refuel. Make

sure your boss, company, and family know that this is non-negotiable. Plan personal days and vacations so that your time is used wisely and productively.

- Live a meaningful life! Every waking moment should be engaged in some form of mental, physical, or emotional human experience. And sometimes you can do all three at the same time. Just doing nothing shouldn't be an option; even if you're relaxing or socializing, make the experience enriching and not a waste of time. Those precious hours will never be reclaimed.

9

Act with Focus, Know When to Edit, and Be Present

> The secret of change is to focus all of your energy, not on fighting
> the old, but on building the new.
> —Socrates (fictional character) in Dan Millman's
> *Way of the Peaceful Warrior*

Modern life can be overwhelming at times. Let's start with the little things, like the deluge of technology that has become part of everyday living: cell phones, laptops, iPads, apps for every service imaginable (from ordering your favorite coffee drink to checking the weather), streaming services, social media platforms, Skype, Zoom, online banking, airline reservations, Dropbox, and on and on. It can be dizzying, especially for people who are not "digital natives."

According to KommandoTech, Americans spend an average of 5.4 hours on their phones every day.[1] Some of these hours may be for work, as well as family needs such as time-saving online shopping. But a lot of that time is spent scrolling and obsessing, which eat up valuable time that could produce a whole lot more value for your waking hours. As much as technology and digital products have simplified some aspects of our lives, they have also made our lives a lot "noisier," which can cause us to lose our focus on what really matters.

When I speak to younger people, I often give them a challenge: no devices for twenty-four hours, no technology of any kind. They look at me in astonishment, as if that isn't even possible. My suggestion to them is to take a walk in the park and look around. Have a face-to-face conversation with a friend. Read a physical book. Or prepare and have a meal with a family member and enjoy it without any phones nearby. My thesis is that all of a sudden, desires will start to surface and will seem much more important than the latest video on YouTube.

> *As much as technology and digital products have simplified some aspects of our lives, they have also made our lives a lot "noisier," which can cause us to lose our focus on what really matters.*

Ironically, a similar challenge could be posed to people forty and older, since many of us also have a digital fixation. Guilty as charged, when I think about how many times a day I check the news on multiple sites, see who has responded to my social media postings, and scroll through emails. It all seems pretty unavoidable in the moment, but the question is *Is this really the best use of my time?* If asked to put digital technology aside for twenty-four hours, could you do it?

ROAR TIP

Do an inventory of your digital activities in a given day, and figure out how much of what you are doing is actually meaningless to your life. Edit, edit, edit. You might be able to recapture an hour a day, times seven days a week, times four weeks—now there are twenty-eight hours you could be using for something that is more important to you.

Not too long ago, I was having a conversation with a former colleague who was recently divorced and was sharing custody of her two school-age kids. Like any busy working mom, her days were packed with responsibilities. Yet she found herself having every other weekend free, when her children were with their other parent. "It's a gift of time," I suggested. "Take those forty-eight hours times twenty-six weeks, and you have 1,248 hours in one year. Call it your 1,248 Project!" I asked her, "How will you use those hours for your own future? Will it be to learn something new for your next career move? To learn how to date again? To expand on a hobby? At the end of the year, what new thing will you have accomplished to move yourself forward?"

When some people get stuck in this process, they turn to meditation or mindfulness, focusing on the intense moment of the present to understand their thoughts and feelings and goals. If that works for you, I say do it daily. We all need to find whatever allows us to formulate what we want and determine how we will go about getting it.

My go-to solution is long-distance running. When I'm out on a country road, focusing on a six-mile run, the world seems to open up to me. I achieve clarity of mind, body, and soul—and the world flows through me. My anxieties disappear, solutions to nagging problems surface in my brain, and I gain insight into what my priorities need to be.

Running is when I talk to myself and to God. I experience the intensity of the present, not only to avoid stepping into a pothole but also when I take in the glory of nature that unveils itself on my run—and I'm thankful that I'm healthy and lucky to be someone who is able to run. When I am running, I'm particularly grateful for my life, my family, and my friends, and I'm conscious of being one with the universe. Running is my happy place, and I do it year-round, in all weather and in all places.

When you run, it is also all about time. Not that I really care about running stats anymore, but of course I do, when I'm focused on breaking two hours for a half marathon or four hours for a marathon. The goal is there and not there, but what is always there is that time for me to be with myself to think about everything. My friend Linda calls it "moving meditation." Time is our precious commodity and once we honor that, it is amazing what we can accomplish.

Time is our precious commodity and once we honor that, it is amazing what we can accomplish.

Running may not be your thing, but what is your thing? What lets you clear your brain and feel at peace with yourself? What can you say brings you joy, and how do you stay focused to keep experiencing what it brings to you?

ROAR TIP

What brings you joy? It might be as simple as sitting on your back porch on a glorious summer day or letting the sun bathe you in its warmth while you putter in your garden. Grab hold of that special feeling and use it as a gauge when doing a self-check on your life's progress.

Time alone on your porch, sailing on a lake, or doing that yoga pose. Being alone in a river with your fishing rod, or hiking that trail, or planting perennials. Do whatever it is that brings you joy and takes you away from the television and your digital life, helping you to get clear on how you can use time in a way that will refresh you. Let inspiration surface to help you answer the question of what you really need to do with your time. Indeed, time is one of the great mysteries of life. Sir Isaac Newton believed that time is absolutely real, while Buddhists believe that time is only a concept in our minds. Are the past and the present all that we really know as a true measurement of time?

Do you lament the time wasted on things in the past? If so, concentrate now on ways to use your precious days more productively in the future. Aside from being alone with yourself to help that process, as I do with running, there is a whole industry around the concept of time management and ways that you can edit your life to maximize what is important to you.

ROAR TIP

Check out *Deep Work: Rules for Focused Success in a Distracted World* by Cal Newport. I love the concept of deep work, as it underscores how you can spend your time on what is most important to you. *Eat That Frog!* by Brian Tracy is another solid choice for advice on how to get the important things done.

My friend Keith follows the OHIO method in regard to his long list of things to do; it stands for "only handle it once." Don't linger on your list. Get it done—from the small, mundane tasks (which can eat up a chunk of your day) to the bigger items that need to be accomplished. Procrastination is the scourge of a productive life.

The Top Five Regrets of the Dying, a book by Bronnie Ware, puts time into perspective, in that it moves at a furious pace. A hospice nurse for decades, Bronnie worked with people spending their last days on earth. She aggregated what she heard from them into five key themes. A lot of what they said was about time, including "I wish I hadn't worked so hard and spent more time with the people who mattered to me."[2] Another theme was "I wish I'd had the courage to express my feelings. No guilt." People waste a lot of time on pleasing others.[3]

We all know people who have a hard time staying on task to get things done. Seminars, speakers, and exercises abound that can help you reorient yourself to a more productive day. One popular idea is the Pomodoro Technique: To reduce the impact of internal and external interruptions to your focus, use a timer to break down work into intervals of twenty-five minutes in length, separated by short breaks. It is a way to bring some discipline into teaching yourself how to accomplish more, and it's never too late to start utilizing this technique.

My own obsession with time management is to use a multicolumn to-do list on a daily basis. It includes work-related tasks, personal things that need to get done (like an exercise regimen), and stuff that seems to suck up an inordinate amount of time, such as getting someone to come to the house to fix the air conditioner. But I'm relentless about crossing as much off the list as possible on any given day. It's become a game I play with myself. The more check marks on a day, the better. I use a green highlighter to cross out what I have accomplished in that day. Those green lines give me a great deal of satisfaction, particularly in the house chores column!

Sometimes to-dos can be bumped into the following year, depending on how much is on the list. I still haven't managed to get to my three last states, North and South Dakota and Nebraska. And although I can speak some French and Italian, I do want to learn Spanish, and though I have started taking classes, I have a long way to go.

Some people have mastered the notion of focus, particularly in mid-life when they realize it is now or never! Cleveland native Don Loftus[4] is one such person. He'd always had an interest in writing plays; from fifth to ninth grade, he cowrote them with his grade-school friend, Mark O'Donnell, the author of *Hairspray* and other notable works. Don got sidetracked from his love of playwriting as he became an accomplished executive in retail and then with other major consumer-goods companies. His work took him around the world as he reached new heights in his profession.

> **ROAR TIP**
>
> As I wrote in an earlier chapter, I'm also obsessed with writing down my goals for any given year. I check on my "life journal" on a regular basis to see how I am progressing. I also keep a three-year list. What is it that I want to accomplish over the next three years? That list keeps me centered on which countries I still want to visit and what new project I'd like to take on, such as starting a graduate school program. Ticking off what I've done on my "life to-do list" keeps me motivated toward finding fulfillment. Give this practice a try–it might work for you too.

Don never lost sight of his first love, and over most of his adult life, he would rise early to write before work, while his wife slept nearby. He even had some of his plays produced in regional theaters along the way.

In his early sixties, Don decided that not only did he have to continue writing and editing his plays, but he needed to edit his life to focus 100 percent on his passion. As he says, he has put his life into hyperdrive. He became involved in the Dramatists Guild Foundation and joined a writing group that meets weekly to read and critique each other's work. He also joined a group of playwrights and actors who meet to read plays. He has fully immersed himself in the playwriting world, editing out other things that don't matter as much to him.

Over two years, Don wrote twenty-nine plays, from dramas to musicals and comedies. He is constantly writing, sometimes moving back and forth between works, writing 90 to 120 pages a week. He has learned how to submit plays to theaters and organizations and producers, clocking in at 1600 submissions in total for fifteen of his plays. The good news is that many of his plays have been produced across the United States, and he is now a bona fide playwright by profession and identification.

"I'm working harder than I ever have but having much more fun. My ultimate goal is to see one of my plays being produced either off-Broadway or on Broadway," he said. Don is someone who knows how to edit, literally and figuratively.

Jeffrey Banks[5] knows a bit about editing too. Jeffrey is a highly successful fashion designer who started his own design business at twenty-two, creating fashion for adults and children. He was the youngest designer to win the prestigious Coty American Fashion Critics' Award and became a known player in the industry.

He learned the value of editing early, since you cannot produce every idea when designing a product line. However, since he was a child, he had had what he would call an obsession with tartan plaid, and he could not, would not "edit" it out of his mind! Jeffrey's research into the topic was coming up short, so he decided he would write a book about plaid. "Never mind that I am not a writer, had never written a book, and did not have a book deal with a potential publisher," he said, explaining that what he *did* have was a desire, a drive, and a belief that somehow, some way, he could do it!

Jeffrey learned from people as far afield as theologians and psychologists, who told him that the lure of tartan is the quest to belong, to a tribe, a clan, a family. He started the book project at forty-nine, and at fifty-four—five years and two editors later—*Tartan: Romancing the Plaid* was born. As he described it, the process was one of the hardest things, professionally, that he had ever gone through. He found a publisher and produced a lush coffee-table book that weighed in at six pounds and six ounces, resulting in him becoming a worldwide expert on the subject of plaid.

That was five books ago. Clearly, Jeffrey's editing skills were at work in a different way, as he left his fashion design life behind and focused on his passion. But the story doesn't end there. During a dinner conversation with his friend Mindy Grossman, who had just become the head of HSN, the shopping network, she told him how much she loved his book and asked if he would think of designing some tartan-centric gifts for the holiday home. After submitting some sketches (edited of course), a full-fledged home decor collection was born, encompassing furniture, rugs, bedding, pillows, candles, crystal, pajamas and robes, and even cookies and cookie jars.

Now in his sixties, Jeffrey has been at it for a decade, including going on-air to sell on a monthly basis. If you are an HSN shopper, you know Jeffrey's work and you see his keen eye for editing. "Did I ever think I'd be doing this? No way," he said, but his advice is to always embrace the new, as you never know where it might take you.

When I spoke with Mike,[6] I thought I had met "my brother from another mother," in that he and I share the ability to be an über-multitasker and what I like to call a lifelong learner.

Mike spent most of his formative years in Birmingham, Alabama. He graduated from college and became an army officer before spending more than thirty years in the food industry, from general management to operations at companies that are household names. Married with children, he was a busy executive, putting in the hours required to become a top player in his field, yet a few things were always lingering at the back of his mind.

One of those was his boyhood dream to become a pilot. For one reason or another, he put it off year after year. But at fifty-seven, he decided that he had to pursue his dream and headed to a flight school to begin the process. "The stars were never going to align, so I had to align them myself," he explained, as he worked toward and obtained his license. The bonus along the way is that his wife joined in and took lessons too. If he hadn't pursued his dream, he may have never become the pilot who he is today. In his sixties now, Mike plans to pilot planes "until the doctor says I can't." He flies around the Midwest from Chicago to Nashville to Oklahoma City on a regular basis for his business and for pleasure.

But Mike has lots of interests to keep himself busy. He wrote a novel that was published and has another one "in the drawer." In 2018, as he was turning sixty, he took an online business application course in AI and robotics at MIT to help his company move into the future, and that has now led to his next big project, a doctoral program at USC in organizational change and leadership. At sixty-two. The course will be three and a half years with no breaks and, of course, a dissertation that he will have to defend.

"I have this constant inner yearning to see what's around the corner," he told me. "Age is just a number to me. Chronology is just a way to describe your experiences to date." His comments reminded me of one of my favorite sayings, expressed by Mahatma Gandhi and others: "Live as if you were to die tomorrow, learn as if you were to live forever."

Mike and his wife love the Nashville area, where he thinks they will settle, but he has a long list of things for after he finishes his doctoral program. He wants to teach, write more fiction, and maybe even start a flight instruction school for individuals who are economically marginalized, as a way to expand on his love of flying. Mike definitely doesn't get overwhelmed with life: he is intent on doing what he enjoys, what's important to him, and he keeps his life tight around those goals.

> **ROAR TIP**
>
> Be honest with yourself. What is holding you back from zeroing in on your dreams? Everyone carries baggage from the past, and everyone can change "I wish I had pursued my talent in . . ." to "My dream is to become . . ." and then make it happen.

Not everyone can be as focused as Mike, but everyone can learn how to fight overwhelm and edit things down to what is most essential to being you. Remember Susan Boyle? At forty-seven, she applied for an audition for *Britain's Got Talent*. If you haven't watched her performance, go to YouTube now and see what you missed. When she sang "I Dreamed a Dream" from *Les Misérables*, she took the show and the world by storm. In 2009, the performance was watched more than 120 million times! She melted our hearts and went on to become a musical superstar with bestselling albums, concert tours, and global recognition. Today, at sixty, she continues to dazzle audiences everywhere.

Step out on your stage and let yourself be heard!

Susan Boyle ROARed into her second half of life, pursuing her dreams in a way that makes her a role model for every single one of us who has doubts and insecurity. Step out on your stage and let yourself be heard!

ROAR: Chapter Takeaways

- Everyday distractions keep people from what I'll call "the focus"—your own truth for what you want. Is it a new career, a new love, a new start somewhere else? Give it the time and attention that it needs, nurture it, and it will grow. Start by having a twenty-four-hour digital-free life. Take a walk in the park. Read a physical book. Have an in-person, face-to-face conversation.

- Do you really need to be on four social media platforms? Why? Step away from some of them, and you'll see that your life will be better. Decide what digital outlets or things you can live without. Edit out the extraneous, the things that bring no true meaning. Start to edit now!

- Try the OHIO method: only handle it once. We all have a list of details that we need to resolve in a given day. Being decisive will save you hours and free you up for more time for family, passion projects, and thinking about how you can ROAR!

- Focus. Focus. After editing what doesn't work for you anymore, attend to what is working. If you have a burgeoning relationship, focus on it fast. It will bring you the most satisfaction in the long run.

PART IV

Reassess Your
Relationships

10

Reassess Your Personal Relationships— with Yourself, Your Family, and Your Friends

Life is change. Growth is optional. Choose wisely.
—Karen Kaiser Clark

We all know that the key to a happy life is the relationship you have with yourself. Every book, podcast, lecture, or meeting that you attend will emphasize that idea. If you are living someone else's life or not being true to your inner compass—your North Star—then you will be stuck. Some people learn this early, yet for others, it takes years to finally get to the place that is right for them.

> *If you are living someone else's life or not being true to your inner compass—your North Star— then you will be stuck.*

One of my secret indulgences is to read self-help books. It started with *What Color Is Your Parachute?*, then Dale Carnegie's *How to Win Friends and Influence People.* My grandmother admired Norman Vincent Peale, so *The Power of Positive Thinking* was a must-read. Each of these books (and more!) gave me hints and insights that helped shape my personal worldview. They affected how I created a relationship with myself, which, in combination with the influence of family, friends, and teachers, made an imprint on my early life.

Fortunately, I was able to set my deep convictions early and focus on what I truly wanted to do with my life. The determination was to get an education and become a success—both in a career and as a human being. But most important, I was determined to understand who I was and who I wanted to become. For some, it comes early. For others, it can take longer. What's important is that we get to that place.

Raised in a Southern Baptist family in rural Virginia, Chuck[1] grew up with the dream of going to college, having a family, and living a comfortable life. In hindsight, he said that a lot of these goals came from his family's expectations of what his life should be like, and he never seriously questioned it. "I was afraid of upsetting the apple cart," he told me. "We were a tight-knit family, and everything was harmonious."

Chuck went on to college, married his college sweetheart, had two kids, and moved to Connecticut. He was living his dream life, commuting to New York City as an executive for a global company, running marathons, and competing in Ironman competitions. He adored his daughters and became the ultimate soccer and lacrosse dad. Life seemed pretty good until he turned fifty.

When his kids grew up and went off to college, he saw his kids had been the important glue keeping his marriage together. He and his wife, as with many couples, had drifted apart, with different dreams and goals. But there was something else gnawing at his inner mind. Since he was a young man, he had always wondered about his sexuality. While he had had many girlfriends, deep in his soul, he knew he had always been attracted to men.

Without the demands of his kids and with the heavy years of building a career behind him, Chuck started to see that maybe he wasn't living the life he should be living. "It was an awakening. I spent a lot of time praying, but I struggled. I knew that God had a plan for me, but I wasn't sure what it was yet," he explained.

In his early fifties, he waited for something to present itself as he thought about what his future might be like. It came to him through a sudden opportunity to rent an apartment in New York, something that he hadn't ever considered. "It was an opportunity, not another person, that saved me," he remembered. From there, his life changed pretty quickly. He and his wife agreed to a separation, and he moved into the city. "It was a massive sense of relief. All of a sudden, I didn't have responsibilities of a house, of kids, of a partner. In New York, you can be whoever you want to be, and I started to think about starting a whole new chapter at fifty-three years old."

Coming to terms with his true self and his sexuality, Chuck began to date men and sensed that this was the right course for him, although he continued to struggle with self-acceptance. One warm summer night he decided to bicycle down to a local watering hole, and there he met Michael. They talked for hours on the outdoor rooftop and began a relationship that is now five years along. "My life is very exciting for me. I have a partner who loves me and vice versa, my work is fulfilling, and my own kids and now grandkids know and love Michael, too. Even my ex-wife and he have become great friends," he laughed.

Chuck is one of the lucky ones, as he not only reassessed his relationship with himself but also with his family—the world he thought he was supposed to live in, and the life he thought he was supposed to lead. He bravely stepped forward into his true self to find a path that has brought him happiness and contentment.

We all know stories like this: The dentist who wanted to be an anthropologist but was talked out of it by his parents. The businessman who wanted to be a social worker, but his wife didn't approve. The lawyer who stepped off her career track to have children—though she wasn't sure she even wanted to be a mother—satisfying what her husband wanted. Too often, we can get sidetracked by others' dreams. At what point do we course-correct to fulfill our own?

It wasn't hard for me to stay true to my own goals. Unlike Chuck, I was never interested in living a suburban life; instead, I wanted to live in a big city. My college girlfriends all wanted a traditional, comfortable life, with the proverbial picket fence and two kids. At an early age, I knew I didn't want that picket-fence life or to be a father, and I've never regretted those decisions. And while I know plenty of suburban parents who love their lives, my posse is composed of likeminded urban dwellers who have the independence that comes with that choice. I stayed the course of my own North Star, and it led me to a life of personal satisfaction. We are all responsible to ourselves for finding inner peace and standing by our convictions, regardless of what anyone else thinks.

We are all responsible to ourselves for finding inner peace and standing by our convictions, regardless of what anyone else thinks.

A woman I once sat next to on a plane asked me, "Who will take care of you in your old age?" when she learned that I had no children. Ironically, this woman's kids live across the country and she hadn't seen either of them in a couple of years, so I asked her the same question. If we know what we truly want, then we construct our lives in a way to have our built-in support systems of family and friends who acknowledge that and who are there for us. I dream about having a big compound with all my friends living together as we age.

Many people who had kids in their twenties are now faced with empty-nest syndrome in their mid-forties. All of a sudden, child-rearing duties are behind them, and they have a lot of free time. They look at the spouse next to them and wonder, *Is that who I want to spend the rest of my life with?* If it isn't, you've got some hard thinking to do and some hard decisions to make.

ROAR TIP

Don't let negative self-talk rule your life. When you catch yourself using it, write it down, read it at the end of the day (when you have time to reflect on why you said it), and then throw it out the proverbial window.

Dr. Anastasia Parsons[2] is a psychologist trained in marriage and family therapy, along with cognitive behavioral therapy (CBT), which is an evidence-based psychological practice widely followed in the US today. It works in the construct that thoughts, feelings, and behaviors are all connected, and if you can change one, you can change all of them.

She explained that many people in their forties and fifties suffer from negative self-talk, such as *I'm not good enough* or *I'm a failure.* This gets louder and picks up speed as we age, becoming its own powerful system in our minds. This can also affect our most intimate relationships. Let's say that someone is in an abusive relationship with their spouse. They can't believe they can do any better, so they let the abuse continue, believing no one else would ever want to be with them.

Dr. Parsons suggested that you focus on those who *do* give you positive feedback, either at work or in other parts of your life. Find evidence that others value you, and then reinforce that in positive self-talk. That cognitive restructuring can help to break through an abusive relationship and let you leave it. For example, if someone gets fired from their job, they might say, *I'm worthless, I'm sad, I'm a failure.* But what if they were actually miserable in that job? If they can view this as an opportunity, a second chance, or newfound freedom, then they have reframed the internal conversation and will feel more in control, more hopeful and confident, possibly leading to a new direction.

Finding meaning for ourselves is critical, as we are all going to have a reckoning about our lives and about our own mortality. "It is a choice how we make meaning in our lives. We all have to have positive self-talk to move forward to create the narrative of our lives," Dr. Parsons said. "If your relationship with yourself is not good, then you won't be any good with anyone else. We are aware of how we talk to people, but less aware of how we talk to ourselves in our own head. We have to talk to ourselves in a kind way, listening to our own tone, the dialog going on behind the scenes."

> *Finding meaning for ourselves is critical, as we are all going to have a reckoning about our lives and about our own mortality.*

According to Dr. Parsons, American society has an unrealistic definition of happiness. As she told me, her belief is that if you are having positive thoughts and emotions at least 51 percent of the time, that will lead to levels of contentment. She also recommends that people create a "self-love book." Fill it with notes or letters or emails that you receive from family, friends, and colleagues praising your accomplishments and what is positive about you. It will reinforce that positive self-talk to build a better relationship with yourself.

We are bombarded with demands from our spouses, kids, family, friends, and colleagues. They all want a piece of us, and most of us want to make everyone who is important to us happy. But we know that is not realistic. You have to say no, or as I like to say, you need to have "no days." So, if your aunt and uncle demand that you come to their annual Christmas party, and you just don't like going there, at what point do you have the courage to say, "I'm not going!"?

ROAR TIP

To align your priorities with reality, you must first gain a clear point of view about your priorities. If you say you want to spend more time with your children, but you spend the majority of your time at the office, you are misaligned with yourself. Dr. Parsons recommends a quarterly check-in. Ask yourself: *How am I spending my time? Is this how I want to spend it? Are your answers in alignment?* If not, you will be headed into crisis at some point. She suggested that you write your questions and answers in a journal, or sit alone for an hour in a quiet place and be honest with yourself.

I hate the concept of brunch, as I mentioned earlier. To me, it is a waste of several hours spent eating and maybe drinking in the middle of the day, when I could be exercising or doing something that is more important to me. For a long time, I went, begrudgingly, whining that I had just wasted four hours listening to a conversation that wasn't that interesting. Finally, I decided I would never do brunch again. I told everyone in my circle to please not invite me, which didn't hurt anyone's feelings—because they all knew how I felt about the B-word! Take control of your time, and let people know what you don't want to do with it.

If you are miserable going to that Christmas party or having to spend every Thanksgiving at your sister's and that is not what you want to do, start by making another plan one year. Going on a trip can be appealing because you can get four or five days over that long weekend. Explain that you want to try a different kind of holiday. She may be hurt at first, but let her know that this is important to you and why she needs to appreciate that. Better yet, invite her to go along.

Remember, your time, your personal time—whether you spend it by yourself or with the people you truly want to be with—should always be in line with your priorities. Once you "train" people that you travel on holidays, or that you don't want to sit for hours and watch yet another game, or that you hate brunch, you will break an undesirable pattern and start a different one that is more meaningful to you. It's okay to be selfish about your time.

One of my favorite examples of someone who took complete control of her time and her life is Michelle Morris.[3] At fifty-two, she had been divorced for ten years, raising four children (including triplets!) as a single mother. For a long period, she had devoted herself to making a living in sales and raising her children, but at fifty-one, she had the recurrent feeling that it was time for a change. "I woke up for months thinking, *How do I want to change, and what do I want to change? I have a huge life of fulfillment behind me, but how do I keep my life enriched moving forward?*"

Like many parents when her kids were off to college, she now needed to face her own future. She decided to create her own "year of change" and to tackle everything all at once: work, lifestyle, personal relationships, and spirituality. She also wanted to rethink money, explaining that raising four kids in the suburbs of Chicago was expensive, so she always had to drive to secure the next sale to earn more money to live on and to save. But was that still her future?

When I heard her story, it reminded me that people like Michelle have perfected the process of change, as her approach is an inspiration to anyone who truly wants to ROAR forward. First, she set off on a professional reset. She had been in her industry for thirty years, but it was changing and she wanted to step out. However, before she did, she spoke to everyone who had had an impact on her career, from her first boss to her favorite colleagues, managers, and clients. She did a complete diagnostic of her industry and the opportunities within it, reaffirming her decision to leave.

She then made a list of all her passions, which included food and wine, home design, and sports. She started meeting with sports teams such as the Chicago Blackhawks and the Bears, and with companies that were in her passion areas, seeing if there might be an opportunity for her to pivot into. At the same time, she sold the six-bedroom house where she had raised her kids. While many traditions and memories were made there, she knew she no longer needed it, not to mention the ongoing costs of landscaping and tax bills. Instead, she rented a small cottage in the same neighborhood, giving her the freedom to be flexible on several fronts.

She looked within herself, gathering the information she needed, listening and learning. She did meditation at night, yoga in the morning, and turned to her religion, attending daily mass and spiritual discipline. "I grew up Catholic and went to Catholic schools through college, so my religion was always important to me, but my relationship with God changed. It was a new trust, and God was now totally guiding and providing, completely without question," she said.

Midway through her year of change, she also hired a life coach named Catherine, after a friend recommended her. They instantly connected, and Catherine helped Michelle formulate her thoughts in a deeper way. "If you follow your passion, success will come," she told her, as Michelle pondered, *What next?*

As she opened herself up to the world and its possibilities during her year of change, she happened to meet a man named Marty, whom she calls her angel, sent by God. She describes him as someone who is always listening, asking great questions, supporting her along the way. "It's the healthiest relationship and the most fun I've ever had," she said, noting that she had been single for ten years. "It's impossible to explain this love, and something I honestly never thought would happen, that now totally completes me," she said.

Ultimately, Michelle moved into an entirely different industry, too, one that is centered on her passion for the home. Her responsibilities include building out the brand's media platforms and much more. She is learning something new every day and thriving in her new job. "I have been told numerous times lately that I seem so happy, and I am truly at peace with myself. I'm ready for the next chapter of my life in my career, in my relationship, in my journey with God, and waking up every day with a drive fueled by passion," she explained.

When it comes to her advice for anyone starting on this new path for themselves, here is what Michelle had to say: "Pull all the weeds out of your life, and your garden will be in full bloom! How can you grow with any weeds?"

While Michelle took it all on in her year of change, you don't have to do the same. But you do need to start somewhere. And it would be extremely difficult to do it alone.

> **ROAR TIP**
>
> Your spouse, children, family, and friends will be your support system in making the changes you need to make to ROAR forward. And you have to make the tough choices about who is on "TEAM YOU"—and who isn't. The best advice is to surround yourself with people who will always support you and have your back, who genuinely care about you, and who are not in any way jealous of you.

As you get older, it's even more important to spend your time with the people who make you happy. A toxic relationship with your mother or sister or child has to be acknowledged and either repaired or stepped away from. That might be a shocking idea, but it is for your own health and well-being. Yes, it's easier with a non–family member, but everyone in your life should be part of this process.

For example, I have an aunt who convinced my grandmother—on her deathbed—to sign over everything my grandmother owned to her only, leaving my aunt's three siblings (including my mother) out of the will. When my aunt did that, I made a decision about my relationship with her. From that day on, I chose not to communicate with my aunt, as I couldn't believe someone in my own family could have such greed in her heart. It was one of the most painful decisions of my life, but it was the right one for me at that time. Ultimately, I forgave her for her actions, as did my mother, but my aunt was never really a part of our family again.

The same goes for friendships. One of my best friends just couldn't get over his jealousy of my achievements, and we had to part ways. The situation was bringing me down, and I would try to rationalize his jealousy or justify the friendship. Although we had great memories together, it became clearer and clearer that this friendship had no future for me.

On the other hand, we know people who love us even with all our faults! Who are the people you know you can rely on, be vulnerable with, bare your soul to, share your insecurities and fears with? That is a precious group of people you should always nurture and be fully present with. My advice is to seek more of those people and make them a part of your tribe.

My own tried-and-true friends always have my best interests in mind—and, by the way, they aren't shy about telling me when I'm wrong or have screwed up. It's also been a gift for me to form new relationships in my sixties with people who fit that bill too, as this should be a lifelong pursuit.

Find people who fill you up. It's never too late to make new friends. Get to know people from various walks of life, who are different from you in some way, who offer a life perspective that's not identical to your own. If nothing else, it makes for stimulating conversations. For me, it's also important to have friends of all ages. I cultivate friendships with people in their twenties and thirties, eighties and nineties, as they all give me fresh perspectives. Don't let your circle of friends shrink as you age—stretch and expand your valued relationships.

ROAR TIP

One of my favorite scenarios to pose is this: *It is the end of your life, and you can only have five people at your bedside. Who will they be?* It's a tough choice but a helpful exercise because it offers a reality check on whom you cherish the most. Think about the five most influential people who have been in your life since your youth. Who helped shape your worldview? Okay, let's make it easier. What five people shaped your worldview up to the age of twenty-one? What five people shaped your view as an adult? Are you in touch with them?

My grandmother was a major influence for me, and I still feel her impact on my thinking to this day. She helped me understand that all things could be possible if you had the vision, stayed positive, and worked for it. I had the perfect mother who was my biggest cheerleader and supporter. She was always there for me in any way. My father is still my sounding board on so many important decisions and taught me how to be responsible and empathetic. Both my parents encouraged my sense of independence and curiosity.

Another encouraging person in my life, one with whom I still correspond, is my high school English teacher, Richard Price, who taught me about books and ideas. I also stay in touch with Carol, one of my high school friends, although we don't see each other that often. We always felt that we were an island unto ourselves because we believed in learning and understanding current events, something that wasn't necessarily the cool thing to do in our working-class high school. To this day, we share books and articles with each other.

If you didn't have that in your life, can you play that role in someone else's life? Maybe it's a young relative, a neighbor, or someone on a team that you coach. Maybe it's another adult who shares your deep-seated interests. The impact of an adult who reinforces a child's best work has enormous consequences for that child's sense of self, especially when you can identify their unique talent or interest. And no matter their age, adults can benefit from that positive reinforcement too.

One of the best pieces of advice I got when I was a young professional was to live the life of the person you want to be, and you will become like that person.

In our adult life, if we have a partner, a boss, or a friend who is there to support us, then we are blessed. They help you to become your true self. Tom is someone I know I can turn to with any problem or vulnerability. He will tell it like it is, and he shares the sharpest insights of anyone I know. For over forty years, he has been my soulmate, always having my best interest in mind and vice versa. One of the best pieces of advice I got when I was a young professional was to live the life of the person you want to be, and you will become like that person. My goal was to be a successful media executive in New York City, to be able to meet and work with interesting and creative people, and to be able to expand my knowledge and experiences through travel and culture. I also wanted to be known as compassionate and loyal and honest—not only to those around me, but as my reputation. I've been lucky to achieve a great deal of that and can say that I have become the person that I wanted to be. Yet there is always room to grow, as I'm far from perfect.

I've already done the work on who I would want at my bedside when my day comes. (I won't reveal their names yet, as I hope we all have a lot more living to do and some may outlive others.) Find your tribe, keep them close, and let them be the wind beneath your wings, particularly in your later years.

ROAR TIP

Here's the next set of exercises to assess your relationship with yourself: *What are the five traits you would use to identify yourself?* Write them down and fold the piece of paper. Then, the next time you are with your tribe of close friends, ask them to tell you the five traits that they would use to describe you. Do they match up with yours? Sometimes, we delude ourselves into thinking that we are one way, and our friends see us another way. It's an enlightening exercise to go through! How do you see yourself with regard to your public persona, and is it the authentic you? Or is it some fabrication of who you think you might be?

I know the five traits I would use to describe myself, and I asked twelve family members and friends, including my dad, to respond to me individually. Nine out of twelve said "generous," eight of them said "focused/determined," and the three other most-named traits were "optimistic," "caring," and "loyal." Those are good enough for me and do match my own perception. Years ago, I wanted to be known as generous in all of the word's interpretations, so it was rewarding to get that feedback. Although I didn't ask for assessment of my negative traits, I will confess to being impatient, at times too rigid or possessive, and occasionally a pain in the butt!

If you want to go even deeper on the subject, I suggest you check out understandmyself.com, created by Dr. Colin DeYoung, Dr. Lena Quilty, and Dr. Jordan B. Peterson. The process they designed will help you understand more about yourself, including your best romantic prospects and the type of job that might best suit you. They have also created a personality scale known as the Big Five Aspects Scale, which includes extraversion, neuroticism, agreeableness, conscientiousness, and openness to experience. Dr. Peterson is a Canadian clinical psychologist and a professor of psychology at the University of Toronto; he developed the program with his colleagues in his lab there.

Getting back to a less-scientific approach, I also like to ask people to identify the words or short phrases that best describe them, with only one minute to answer. In other words, don't overthink it. How do you define yourself? For me (in no particular order), I would say "adventure traveler," "media man," "best friend," "family man," and "photographer/writer."

When you have become acquainted with who you are, your glow will be sensed by those around you.

Having a reality check with yourself is important. If the traits assessment doesn't match up to your own self-perception, it's time to regroup. If you have a hard time identifying your five descriptors within one minute, you need to do some work with yourself. When you have become acquainted with who you are, your glow will be sensed by those around you. The universe will bring things to you that you didn't expect, whether it is a job, a relationship, or an experience that will move you forward in your life's journey.

ROAR: Chapter Takeaways

- Start by assessing your relationship with yourself. What are the five traits you would use to describe yourself? Do they match up with how your family, friends, and community would describe you? And if there are traits that you want to develop in yourself, identify them and work on strengthening them one at a time.
- Get rid of negative self-talk. Write it down when you have that overly self-critical thought. Read it at the end of the day and ask yourself why you said it. Is it a recurring thought? Where is it coming from? Break it down and then break it up and get rid of it.

- Similarly, keep out negative people. Surround yourself with those who love and support you. With their positive force, you will have the support team in place to help you to ROAR into the person you are destined to be.
- Your personal time is yours to embrace. Be selfish about who you spend it with and what you spend it on. Learn to say no to things that you don't want to do. It will liberate you to have more time to do what matters to you with the people you care about.
- Find your tribe! Surround yourself with the people who support and celebrate you! Make new friends at every age, but make sure you stretch to younger and older people, not just those your own age. Get fresh perspectives. My approach is to have friends from their twenties to their nineties!
- Think about the people who have been the most important influencers on your life since you were a child. Can you identify them? Are they still important to you? Have you thought about reaching out to say thank you?

11

Reassess Work and Your Work Relationships

Keep some room in your heart for the unimaginable.
—Mary Oliver

For the majority of us, work will dominate our lives in one form or another, whether you are an hourly worker who puts in forty hours a week, a part-time employee, a freelancer, or a hard-driving professional or executive who puts in sixty or more hours a week. Whatever your level of engagement, work and what we are paid for it is the fuel that allows us to live the life we want to live or hope to live in the future. Yet when asked, "If you could have any job you wanted, would it be the one you currently have?" 41 percent of the ROAR Into survey respondents said no. And 34 percent said that if they could do it all over again, they wouldn't choose the same career path. Those percentages may seem high, but I would argue that they represent a significant amount of people who seem dissatisfied.

Perhaps the real sentiment came from the question, "If you never had to work again, would you quit your current job today?" Fifty-eight percent of all respondents said yes, and 61 percent of those between ages forty-five and fifty-nine, in mid-career, said yes. It's probably not going to happen, but there sure is a lot of daydreaming about the idea of it.

A significant number of triggers can cause you to step back and look at your work life. They might include disillusionment with your company or management; a desire to get off the corporate treadmill;

a realization that you are on the wrong career track or choice and you need to course-correct; an illness that makes you rethink your life; or you may have been downsized or pushed out, forcing you to design a new future. The reasons for work–life reassessment are myriad, but the important thing is to ask yourself if you are happy with what you are doing and who you are doing it with!

The important thing is to ask yourself if you are happy with what you are doing and who you are doing it with!

At mid-career, you've pretty much figured out what it is that you do and how you do it, and hopefully, you have become pretty good at it. But if you are miserable, what's your plan to change? The same can happen toward the end of your primary career, as you reimagine.

My friend Valerie explained that she spent three years trying to re-create a scenario that was similar to her highly successful executive life, once she retired. When she accepted that it wasn't possible, she found a new path as an executive coach and mentor to other women who were developing their own career paths in business. Her knowledge and experience were indispensable, and today she is thriving in a completely new career that brings her joy and satisfaction.

> **ROAR TIP**
>
> At work, we spend a lot of time with colleagues. It's important to learn to like and respect them, whether they are above you, next to you, or in more junior roles.

When I think about my own work relationships, I've had a few amazing bosses like Jack, Cathie, and David (and I've had a few whom I prefer to forget about). My favorite bosses had impressive vision and leadership skills and empowered me to do my best work. They were also admired by the organization and the industry. Jack was my early-career mentor, who helped me get my first publisher job. Ultimately, I followed him into the executive suite and then as board member and chairman of the Magazine Publishers of America. To this day, he is a mentor and a friend.

In our thirty-five-year friendship, he has always been there to give me the straight talk on career and life. Needless to say, having mentors like Jack, who always have your best interests in mind, is priceless. I would also recommend "reverse mentoring" in your work life. Talk to those twentysomethings in the office to get their point of view, their ideas, and an understanding of what is important to them. Their input will help you see the world in a fresh way and will allow you to grow.

Ultimately, we all have good bosses and not-so-good bosses. Stick with the ones who believe in you and adopt them as your mentors, regardless of where you are in your career. Those relationships will be the ones that let you grow in new and sometimes unexpected ways. If you are stuck with a not-so-good boss right now, figure out how you can navigate away from that person with a new assignment or even a new company. No one should tolerate a situation that is unfair or an environment that is not based on collaboration or transparency. Fortunately, we live in a time when more and more employees are calling out bosses who don't fit that bill.

My great bosses allowed me to hire the best in the business who were my own direct reports. As a result, I had the best publishers in the industry on the team, and they, in turn, hired the best people under them. The culture we fostered was one of teamwork, fairness, and respect for the individual. As they say, it all starts at the top. Sometimes companies can get sidetracked with bad management. Acknowledging a fast course correction is in the best interests of an organization, its culture, and its people. I've watched companies lose their special luster with the wrong people at the helm, resulting in the loss of focus, belief in the mission, and talent—all of which can destabilize a company.

In a world of ongoing change and upheaval, be aware of self-proclaimed "disruptors." They are oftentimes destroyers of companies, institutions, and brands, and especially of older talented employees. Ultimately, respect for seasoned and knowledgeable professionals is what makes a business stronger. Don't fall for the "you are afraid of change" accusation from someone who doesn't respect your expertise.

Here are my five management tips for building effective business relationships with teams—in my case, a group that drove over $1 billion in annual revenue.

1. **Listen.** Sometimes people just need someone to listen to them, so they feel that they are being heard and can be vulnerable without any repercussions. By listening, you'll develop an open and honest relationship with no business surprises, solving issues together.

2. **Be honest.** If someone isn't doing a job to their fullest, explain it to them and see if they agree. If they aren't going to get the promotion, sit down and tell them. If you are going to change their assignment or take pieces away from them, sit down and explain why. People may not be happy, but they will be grateful that you took the time to explain it.

3. **Evaluate people objectively.** We all have numbers next to our names. In any business, we have to deliver the goals, the budgets, the revenues, the profits. It's that simple. Rule by results, not by favorites or cliques or some agenda that is off the focus. Create opportunities for the need of the business, not for the need of an individual.

4. **Treat everyone with respect.** My boss Cathie had a brilliant line: "You treat the most junior member of the team with the same respect that you give the CEO." That has always served me well. When I think about the incredible influence that a CEO's assistant can have with the boss, it can never be underestimated. But more important, it's the right thing to do. Everyone deserves dignity. A zero-tolerance environment for bullying, bad behavior, or treating people disrespectfully should be what every company and manager foster.

5. **Stay humble.** When I was a thirty-four-year-old publisher of *GQ*, I felt pretty full of myself. A senior colleague reminded me that it was all about the seat I was sitting in; it wasn't about me. I never forgot that and have passed that wisdom on to many people who, as my grandmother would say, "got a little too big for their britches." Remember that most of us are hired hands,

whether we are the big boss or not. I was incredibly fortunate in my business life to meet presidents George W. Bush and Barack Obama, celebrities such as George Clooney, Beyoncé, and Barbra Streisand, and sport stars such as Michael Jordan and Serena Williams. But it was the seat I sat in that afforded me those special moments, and I was always grateful for the opportunities.

ROAR TIP

If you don't have a team that reports to you, then take my five management tips and turn them inside out. Does your manager bring these ideas to the workplace? It will foster effective business relationships, producing excellent work. And use those tips in working with your colleagues. You'll develop a reputation as someone whom people want to be around to work on projects and help solve business problems.

The people you have around you can make or break your success, your promotions, your raises, your ability to save more money for your future, and your overall well-being in your current workplace. Surround yourself with positive people who focus on innovation and results. No matter what stage you are at in your career, you can always learn something and grow into another role or assignment. Stay out of office politics and away from divisive, toxic environments. This all sounds like common sense, but step back and assess your situation.

The people you have around you can make or break your success, your promotions, your raises, your ability to save more money for your future, and your overall well-being in your current workplace.

I would be remiss if I did not tell you about an amazing woman named Francine Crane. For thirty-three years, she has been my executive assistant. We met when she was a young, single woman who lived in Brooklyn. From the beginning, she wanted to be an assistant, even though over the years I pushed and prodded to get her on a track where she might do different things. But she had other ideas; among them putting her family life first. She and Harold raised three amazing daughters, all college graduates now pursuing their own careers.

Fran is smart, competent, funny, always one step ahead of me in everything, and I can't even imagine what I would have done without her brilliance. As comfortable talking to Bruce Springsteen as to any major client or elected official on Capitol Hill, Fran endears herself to everyone.

She played that perfect role if someone had bad news and would ask, "Is he in a good mood today?" and would always be my go-to resource for a commonsense understanding of a person or a situation. She would cut right through it with an observation that would astound me. *Why didn't I think of that?*

Often, I would call Fran "my sister from another mister," and I know we will be there for each other to the end. Ours has been one of the best work relationships I have had in my business career.

Being happy at work makes a huge difference in your life, especially in giving you a clear head about how you want to grow there or how you want to pivot to a new place. Sometimes the best way to think about change is when things are going well, which actually gives you the time to make a major change, the one that has been gnawing at you.

I learned about Marc Kaplowitz[1] from his wife, Marla, someone I knew through business. When I told her about the concept for this book, she said, "You have to meet my husband!" Marc was on an amazing track. He had studied business at the University of Michigan, earned an MBA at New York University, worked in finance at companies like Standard & Poor's and Arthur Andersen, did a stint in risk management, and was heading for the senior-most jobs in his industry.

But when he was in his mid-forties, a few things happened. His dad had been a major influence in Marc's life, and when he passed away, Marc began to think about his relationship with work in a different way. He was good at what he did, but he had no passion for it. Luckily, Marc had a strong relationship with his boss and opened up about his desire to transition out of his business. They constructed a plan together that gave Marc the runway to set himself up for what would come next.

"Fortunately, my wife made a good living," Marc told me, "so she was a big contributor for our two kids and me. I started to think about my desire for some type of public service, as it was always a dream before I jumped right into the corporate world. I had volunteered with an agency to help people who struggled after the last recession, and I kept circling back to the idea of how much I loved teaching."

In his late forties, Marc thanked his boss, left his company, and enrolled in a two-year master's program in adolescent education, graduating when he was forty-nine years old. "Going back to school may have also literally saved my life." Marc had had an intense pain in his upper chest, had gone to the emergency room, and was released. In the next month or so, his sixty-year-old professor told the class that he needed to take a leave of absence due to a burning that the professor himself had in his upper chest. Marc suspected that he was having the same symptoms and went to his own doctor. There he found out that he had significant coronary blockages, which led to three stents! Without the professor mentioning it in class, Marc may have missed an important health signal.

With his health stabilized and a fresh degree in hand, this Wall Streeter headed to a New York City public middle school in East Harlem to teach algebra. Today, in his mid-fifties, Marc has found his passion in work and in life. He wants to spend his time on education inequity, noting that so many of the 1.1 million kids in New York City public schools don't even know what possibilities exist for them through education. He does one-to-one tutoring in math, works with inner-city kids on testing capabilities, and feels that he is making a huge contribution to many young lives. Marc's work life is now quite different than his first twenty years, but he would tell you that taking the leap to follow your heart is more invigorating than gutsy.

Another daring person I spoke to is Stephanie Young,[2] who studied English in college and decided to move to New York to pursue a career in publishing. She worked as a copywriter, writer, and editor in the health space, carving out a well-respected niche for herself. As she built her profession, she married and had two children, leading the busy life of a working mom. At fifty-one, Stephanie woke up one morning and questioned whether this was what she was destined to do.

"I liked what I was doing and the people that I worked with, but something told me that it wasn't enough," she said. Over the next six months, she explored every possibility, saving her money for a day when she would decide to do something else and have a nest egg to pursue it. "I cut out my Starbucks habit, didn't buy new clothes, and did some freelance work to augment my next-chapter fund." Nothing excited her until one day when she took a walk with her best friend, who had been to see a life coach. The coach had asked her friend, "If money is not an issue and failure is not an option, what would you like to do?" While her friend kept coming up short, Stephanie blurted out, "To go back to school and become a doctor!" It was her *aha* moment, and it would have lots of twists and turns to it.

She began taking classes that she paid for out of her savings, and learned that she had to take at least eight more classes in subjects like biology, chemistry, and physics. "Luckily I had a relative that worked at a local university and was able to get some tuition discount to help me afford it," she explained. She was fifty-three when she took the MCAT, the boards needed to apply to medical school. "I did pretty well, but I soon learned that American medical schools thought that someone my age was too old to be admitted." Not to be discouraged, she ended up applying to a school in the Caribbean and was accepted for a three-year program. At the same time, Stephanie's marriage was unraveling, her kids were in college, and she decided to, as she put it, "leap off the cliff." What she learned along the way is that there are scholarships and grants and loans available to students of every age. The trick is to be meticulous about the paperwork when searching for assistance.

There are Federal Pell grants, Federal Supplemental Educational Opportunity Grants (FSEOGs), and scholarships offered by schools, regardless of your age. But if you decide that a full degree program is not what you want, look up MOOCs, which stands for Massive Open Online Courses. Most of these courses are free—from Ivy League schools to trade schools, the options are endless. Or check what is available in your state. For example, in Virginia, the Senior Citizens Higher Education Act of 1974 allows residents older than sixty to take college courses for credit at no cost. They must have an annual income of less than $23,850.[3] The Senior Adult Scholarship Program in Alabama allows seniors older than sixty to attend two-year colleges for free. All it takes is some research through sources like ScholarshipOwl.

If you say that you cannot afford going back to school, you are not doing the work to make it happen, as there is a lot of untapped money at your disposal. Stephanie graduated from medical school in her late fifties, but she had to put the pursuit of a residency on hold when she left for California to care for her terminally ill mother. While Stephanie's medical education was helpful during her mother's last year, she reverted to working freelance copyediting and writing jobs.

During that time, she wondered if she would actually practice medicine someday, or if she should think about teaching in a medical college or find work in biotech or as a chief information officer for a medical facility. In order to explore options, she took an online master's course in medical education (fully paid through a scholarship from a university in Scotland). It led her to acknowledge that she didn't really want to teach, but in fact, she wanted to practice medicine. Before you can apply for a medical residency, however, you have to pass the United States Medical Licensing Examination (USMLE).

"I failed the first time, but then did well the second time. I've now applied for residencies in every state, except Florida, and hope to do one in family medicine," Stephanie explained. Now in her early sixties, she is ready to take another leap when an acceptance comes through. Starting again in a new place is now something she's used to, so she is willing to move anywhere for the next step in her journey to becoming a practicing doctor—for the rest of her life. "You can't read about the top ten most beautiful futures," she told me. "You have to find it for yourself, keep the vision, even when you stumble along the way." That *aha* moment in the park, her moment of truth, was over ten years ago.

How many people do you know who would have the courage to do what Stephanie has done? Would you have the courage to take the leap? And the persistence to see things through? If you believe in the ROAR manifesto, you will!

I'm always intrigued with people like Marc and Stephanie, who have it in them to actually ROAR into a brand-new place that means starting from scratch to get on a new path. My friend Walter Cain[4] is a man who was a huge success in his business, but as he said, "I didn't grow up dreaming about being a partner in a private equity firm!" According to Walter, after nearly thirty years in the industry, he did a deep soul search and decided to follow a dormant passion: to become an architect.

ROAR TIP

While it may not be your aspiration to go back to school for a new career, there are lots of sources to explore new career options with your current skills—from Workforce50.com to SeniorJobBank.org. The US Department of Labor website is another source, along with "The Complete Guide to Career Change after 50" on LearnHowToBecome.org. There's also a high demand for electricians and carpenters, and many labor organizations, such as the International Brotherhood of Electrical Workers (IBEW), offer labor apprenticeships.

He had been an English major in undergraduate school and had an MBA from the University of Pennsylvania. He looked for programs that would suit his needs, ultimately deciding on Columbia University, or as he said, they decided on him!

Walter quit his job and became a full-time student again, at fifty-three, to pursue his master's in architecture, planning, and preservation, with an emphasis on sustainable architecture. Upon graduating from the three-year program, he went to work for a design and technology company before launching his own design company, which works in the sustainability space. One of his exciting projects was the 2018 demolition of a space in New York City. Using the resulting thirty-six tons of detritus or debris, he created a pop-up art exhibit called *Demo-Demo* that utilized all the materials and was later recycled for the renovation of the space.

At sixty, Walter is thriving in the world that he created for himself with that big decision in his mid-fifties.

Allison Kluger's[5] is another story of self-invention in a way that was not only genius in its making but also created its own mini-movement. She spent years in the television business at *Good Morning America*, *The View*, and a global shopping network, before she and her husband moved west so he could attend a graduate program at Stanford. In her mid-to-late thirties, she tried a variety of experiences in e-commerce, interactive television, the Al Gore network called Current TV, and more. During that time, she had nine in vitro fertilizations (IVF), as she and her husband hoped to start a family. She became pregnant at forty and again at forty-one and decided to stay home for seven years to raise their two boys.

In her late forties she reassessed her work life and the relationships she had built while raising her sons. For her, it came down to understanding what she calls her "superpowers." "I had to figure out what I was really good at. I knew I had talent in thinking in innovative ways, in imagining and how to relate to people," she said. "We are all an amalgam of every experience that we have had in our life. Think back. Even if you were a Boy Scout or an athlete or did community theater, those skills lie dormant and never go away! Write down everything that you have ever done and figure out what skills fall under each of them. Go back and circle the words that keep popping up. A successful pivot or reimagined life is accessing all of the strengths you have in repackaging yourself," she advised.

As she did this exercise herself, Allison came up with the idea to teach a course, one that would bring in leaders from business and the media world, people she knew as mentors and leaders. She wrote up the course guidelines and shopped it around, particularly to Stanford. It took her three tries, but she persisted, continuing to edit the offering and strengthen its appeal. She landed her first course, on the mastery of communications, at the Stanford Business School. She was forty-seven, armed with a bachelor's degree and a compelling idea.

Today, Allison's courses—Strategic Communication, Reputation Management: Strategies for Successful Communicators, and Strategic Pivoting for Your Next Chapter—are some of the most popular courses on campus. In addition, she was the creator and lecturer of Project You: Building and Extending Your Personal Brand, a course she teaches with Tyra Banks, as well as a course on executive presence for women. In her mid-fifties, Allison's reimagined life has led her to a consulting practice in the field of executive presence and personal branding, areas that she now has a national and international reputation in.

"I've never been happier; my life is more purposeful. I get better and better at it. It feels more like me than anything else I've done. I know I'm an educator, living my true self," she told me. Her best advice is to have a conscious thought process about where you want to go. You might have to mourn the person that you were to get to your new self. "Walk the walk in the direction that you want," she told me.

In my conversation with Allison, I told her that she needs to take her knowledge and teachings to everyone. How about a book? A podcast? A tour that will inspire people to find their strategic reimagination! Something tells me that we will hear a lot more about Allison in years to come. Not only did she talk the talk, but she walked the walk to a whole new place—from scratch.

> **ROAR TIP**
>
> My idea for everyone who is interested in changing their relationship with work is to get ahead of it. Build a parallel life that you can move into when that time comes, without necessarily giving up on your current life. It can take two years, but you can start it anytime.

I began to think about and plan my parallel life in the year 2000, a full twenty years before I left my publishing career, but a lot happened at work that kept me engaged and excited. The magazine industry was changing at a rapid pace, and I needed to keep pace with it, as well as bring along the team. Fortunately, we accomplished a lot, always growing our revenue and profit along the way. We had great support from our CEO, Steve Swartz, who always allowed us to invest in our business. While many of our competitors floundered, we excelled. It also didn't hurt that I got to go to the Golden Globes, the Super Bowl, and the White House Correspondents' Dinner as part of my work perks! Being in the magazine business had exposed me to some of the brightest and most accomplished people in the world. Doing business with the CEOs of major companies also gave me a front row seat to many industries and how they worked. But I started thinking way out into the future, and I knew that I somehow needed to reclaim my interests in writing and photography. I wanted to cultivate them and build a portfolio that would layer on itself, so that when the day came, I could step out of my publishing career and have a completely different life.

When that time came and I had a Wikipedia page set up, it defined me as a writer, photographer, and former magazine publishing executive. It was as if I had shed one skin to take on another, and I have a long list of accomplishments as proof of my transformed identity.

There are many ways to create your parallel life. Follow a passion and build on it. Go back to school, like Marc and Walter did. Create something from scratch while you are raising your kids, or finally chase that entrepreneurial dream, that powerful idea, as Allison did. The key is to figure out what it is that you want to do, and start building the new you on the side. In the ROAR Into survey, when asked, "Do you think you have room in your life to add a new venture?" 66 percent of the respondents said yes, which means they have the intent. When asked, "Do you have talents, skills, and interests you feel you have never explored?" more than 50 percent of all respondents said yes, while 60 percent of those age forty-five to forty-nine said yes. If you answered yes to those questions, therein lies the opportunity to find your parallel self, but you have to put in the work.

It may mean that you stay in your company, or it may mean that you step out toward a new horizon. You may start on a path at fifty-five, then at seventy refire again for a "third half" of your life. Reimagination should never end. Work, in its many definitions, is something we should always be doing in some form. It keeps us vibrant, connected, and relevant. *Refire* is the operative word, and work should never fully stop.

At eighty-five, Alan Patricof, an investor in start-ups, has targeted aging Americans with his latest fund, Primetime Partners. This venture-capital fund focuses on baking early-stage platforms and products for older people and investing in older entrepreneurs with fresh ideas. Debut novelist Delia Owens wrote her blockbuster, *Where the Crawdads Sing*, just as she was turning seventy. It has sold more than 4.5 million copies, and in 2019—only a year after it debuted—it had sold more print copies than any other title, fiction or nonfiction. It was number one for 2019 on Amazon's list of most sold books in fiction and topped the *New York Times* bestseller list for over one hundred weeks. I'd say Delia ROARed into a new kind of work, with hopefully more novels to come for all of us to enjoy in the future. There are other examples too. Not only did Frank McCourt write *Angela's Ashes: A Memoir* in his early sixties, he also won a Pulitzer Prize for it!

With all of us living longer, we have the opportunity to have multiple careers—all it takes is imagination.

With all of us living longer, we have the opportunity to have multiple careers—all it takes is imagination. My friend Penny Ekstein-Lieberman,[6] a successful toy inventor, created Pillow People, the first pillow doll that was a big hit across the country. Her hit product line spawned a short film called *Pillow People Save Christmas*, which you can still see on YouTube. As she approached her seventies, she embarked on a whole new career, producing documentaries on topics that were important to her. The first one featured Israeli American violinist Itzhak Perlman. Already playing violin as a three-year-old, Perlman was stricken with polio at age four, yet he overcame its crippling effects and went on to be the world's most famous violinist. The opportunity arose when she was seated next to him at a dinner and was inspired by his story. Penny had never been involved in creating a documentary before but decided to learn—and then jumped in headfirst.

As an executive producer, you have to come up with a unique film idea, raise the money to make it, follow the budget, find distribution, and address scores of other details. For Penny, it was learning on the job! What did she learn? To work with people you trust, who are in sync with you; to hire an experienced director, producer, and editor who know about documentaries; and to make sure that everyone has the same idea for the production!

After working through her first production, she then embarked on two others: *Dead Reckoning*, a film about war crimes against humanity, and *Inheritance: Women, BRCA, and Hereditary Cancer*, a film that educates people about the deadly breast cancer gene, BRCA. She partnered with award-winning director Jonathan Silvers for both of these films, which aired on PBS.

Now in her seventies, Penny has a separate career as an executive producer of documentaries. She has learned how to develop a concept, collaborate with the right people, raise the $500,000 or more that it takes to produce a documentary, and find the right place for it to air. Alice Walker, author of *The Color Purple* and many other novels, poems, and short stories, said it best: "If you fall in love with the imagination, you understand that it is a free spirit. It will go anywhere and it can do anything!"[7]

Starting something new at any age is the key to unlocking what can be a lifetime of different and fulfilling careers.

Hopefully, we will all live long and prosperous lives that enrich us with our chosen work, whether it is for money or for fulfillment. Starting something new at any age is the key to unlocking what can be a lifetime of different and fulfilling careers. It doesn't matter how many years you will be able to devote to an idea—what matters is that you are passionate about it and that you put in the time to let it flourish. At that point, you won't even call it work, or refer to your ties with others as work relationships. It will be more like a life calling of purpose.

ROAR: Chapter Takeaways

- Work! The very word can conjure up an array of emotions. How do you feel about your work and workplace right now? Are you on the path you want to be on, or is it time to course-correct? Can you do that within your company, or is it time to move on?

- We all have a boss, and many of us manage people. Have you built the reputation of being fair, honest, empathetic? These core values will help to propel your performance, reputation, and ability to grow. Ask five colleagues to describe you. Make sure to ask people above you, people at your level, and more junior associates. Do their descriptions all line up?

- Is it time to close out a twenty-five-year career and start something new? What's the plan? Is it to start your own business?

Make a radical move into another profession? You can do that at fifty and have another twenty-five-year run! Start planning at least two years before you make any change.

- Work means money, and money means work. Sometimes you may have to take one step back to go two steps forward. If you are fortunate in that money is not your issue, then what are you waiting for? At a certain point, the experience and quality of work are more important than the pay. You may be happier making 20 percent less but enjoying the work more. Can you make the change?

12

Reassess Your Community and Your Relationship with It

Twenty years from now you will be more disappointed by the
things you didn't do than by the ones you did do.
—H. Jackson Brown Jr.

Do you feel a responsibility to the world around you? To the people you interact with on a daily basis? Or even to people you don't know?

For most people, "community" means family, friends, and neighbors, or social organizations that they belong to as a way of feeling connected. But community has a broader importance, and that is with our service to each other through engaging with civic activities, nonprofits and their missions, our places of worship, and our commitment to the well-being of each other in all its forms. My friend Martha said that in addition to talking about Social Security, we should add into the conversation the idea of a "secure social community." How do we all become responsible for each other, creating harmony and understanding as fellow citizens and humans? By doing the right thing.

How do we all become responsible for each other, creating harmony and understanding as fellow citizens and humans? By doing the right thing.

We live in a time of significant distrust and unhappiness with the institutions that are supposed to be important to our overall well-being.

In a Pew Research Center survey of 10,618 adults conducted in late 2018, a majority believe that the public's confidence in the US government and in each other is shrinking. The good news, however, is that an overwhelming majority think improvement is possible when it comes to the confidence Americans have in each other: 69 percent of Americans reported they have confidence in others to do the right thing in civic life to help those in need.[1] I witnessed this many times, such as when New Yorkers rallied for each other during the 9/11 terrorist attacks and helped each other after Hurricane Sandy and during the COVID-19 crisis.

The Pew study examined interpersonal trust as well as institutions and other points of view. Fifty-eight percent of adults said they were not confident that others could hold civil conversations with people who have different views.[2] The beauty of American democracy—and democracies in other countries—is that we have the right to express ourselves, and although not everyone might agree, it is important to have the debate and find common ground. As individuals, we may disagree on certain social, economic, or policy issues versus others in our neighborhood, in our workplace, or among our family members, but we need to learn to respect them, regardless of whether we agree with them.

In January 2020, the Edelman Trust Barometer identified government, business, media, and nongovernmental organizations as all having eroding trust from people. Basing trust on two distinct attributes—competence (delivering on promises) and ethical behavior (doing the right thing and working to improve society)—all four institutions fell short.[3] With business, it is the concern of losing jobs to downsizing, a lack of skills, automation, foreign competition, and more, creating a level of uncertainty about the future. More and more studies continue to show that we are a nation of distrust, with no real solutions in sight. But I'm optimistic that a new breed of leaders will be less partisan, reach across the aisle, and work together for a common good.

Many people have entered public service late in life, as a way to contribute to the community. Both Ronald Reagan and Arnold Schwarzenegger won a first-time election as governors of California when they were in their mid-fifties. Alan Webber, former editorial director and cofounder of the magazine *Fast Company*, became a first-time elected official at sixty-nine, when he became the mayor of Santa Fe, New Mexico, defeating three members of the city council and a member of the school board.

> **ROAR TIP**
>
> It's never too late to get involved and contribute to your community, your state, and your country. Start by researching and finding a local organization where you can volunteer–and see where that leads you.

You may not have the aspiration to become governor of your state, but you can still get involved with your local government to improve things in your community. When fifty-six-year-old Bob Oldakowski, a financial controller by profession, relocated from New York to Key Biscayne, Florida, he decided to run for Village Council. He was prompted by a neighbor who had seen Bob in action on his condominium board. After a four-year term on the council, he ran for mayor. And he won two back-to-back terms, the first when he was sixty. During his tenure, he was able to get a community center built for the residents, have the main street redesigned (and paid for by the county) to make it more contemporary, and a lot more. Even as a late-blooming community activist, Bob made major contributions to his fellow citizens.

More and more people are motivated to run for office—of any level—to try to work from within the system to build back more trust and find better solutions from our government, whether federal, state, or local. Maybe you are someone who can step forward to help us build a better future together.

Ginny Donohue[4] is a remarkable woman. At fifty-one, and after working as a CFO in the corporate world, she decided to take a leap. She had begun to volunteer in her upstate New York area to help kids, particularly homeless kids, get into college. Watching the impact that she could have on changing someone's life, she decided to step out after eight years of dedicating herself as a volunteer for the cause.

Ginny quit her job and founded On Point for College in 1999. She told me that with no funds and working out of her car, she visited local settlement houses, Boys & Girls Clubs, and community centers to identify kids who wanted something more from life but didn't understand how to get a college education.

According to Ginny, On Point for College has helped more than 8,700 kids go to college, overcoming the barriers that they face in higher education. It has become a major example of what can be done and is recognized across the country as a beacon of possibility for young people.

So how did Ginny do it? She had a vision, a drive, a purpose, and nothing would hold her back. "There was never a Plan B," she explained. It was in her soul to make this her life's calling.

In the second year of On Point for College, she met Sam Rowser, who shared her passion for helping young people achieve, and they joined forces on the mission. As she described it, all of a sudden they were helping fifty, then a hundred kids, then more. She told me serendipitous things kept happening as the word got out. Donations would arrive at just the right moment from the local community, businesspeople, and more. They aligned with other agencies, such as United Way, and over time, Ginny said the organization built what is now a $2.4 million operating budget dedicated to its cause.

On Point for College's goal is to help kids—from the early stages of understanding the college application process to helping them get every dollar possible from federal and state sources, as well as assistance with housing, textbooks, and transportation. Ginny said they have worked with existing communities, as well as within the refugee community that has settled in the Syracuse–Utica region of New York. As the organization grew, it received grants and funding from companies such as Microsoft, the Kresge Foundation, the New York State Higher Education Services Corporation, and others.

There are twenty-five employees in the organization, and now at age seventy-three, Ginny can step back and look at the extraordinary contribution she has made from what was her dream. When her corporate boss asked her why she was leaving to pursue this goal, her response was, "I need to do something important." The turning point, she said, was when one of the young people whom she was helping said, "Because of you, I'm going to have my dream."

Originally, Ginny's own dream was to help one thousand kids. "God had bigger dreams than I did," she said, laughing, as the organization is now closing in on the nine thousand mark. With that reimagined life working well, Ginny has now tapped into her inner creativity and has become a landscape painter. "My son-in-law bought me $15 worth of paint, and I went on the internet to start learning techniques. I paint two or three times a week now," she said.

When Ginny told me that story, it reminded me of Grandma Moses, the American painter who started painting at seventy-seven, selling her works for $5 a painting. In 2006, her painting *Sugaring Off* sold for $1.2 million.[5] Grandma Moses lived until she was 101 years old, which means that her painting career lasted twenty-four years. Who knows where Ginny's painting will take her?

Another form of community service was conceived by my former colleague Lesley Jane Seymour.[6] Lesley had been a very successful editor in chief of various magazines, including *Marie Claire*, *Redbook*, and *More*, but like many people in the magazine publishing industry, she found herself wondering about what might be next for her.

When *More* magazine was closed by the company that published it, she was forced to think hard about her next play. She had always been interested in science, and in her late fifties, she started taking classes in sustainability and environmental issues, thinking that it might be where she would spend her time in the future. "If you are a lifelong learner and that's who you are, you are always looking for ways to stretch your mind. Going back to school opened up my brain. If you have an opportunity, do it, as it gives you new ways to think," she told me.

Yet a funny thing happened on the way to what would be a master's degree in the subject (after six years of taking classes!). The readers of *More* had been devoted followers of the magazine and were angry and upset when the magazine closed. Lesley decided to tap into that, and she found a way to send out a fifty-four-question survey that she reported brought in 627 responses. What she learned was the incredible need and demand for women to learn from other women. To be inspired and to be informed. She put some money into a developmental project that would tap into her question, "How do I help other women be the best that they can be?"

From there, CoveyClub was born, an online club for women forty and up who want to continue learning, growing, and expanding their world by making new friends and creating deep connections. A covey is a small flock of birds, as Lesley wanted to create a small, cozy, and intimate group with the club's members. Today, several years after she founded CoveyClub, the flock is thriving. There are more than five thousand women on her mailing list. They receive newsletters and have access to exceptional content that appears on the site. According to Lesley, there are five to six webinars a week, Zoom conversations, and—pre-COVID-19—real-life gatherings that will start up again in the future. She said that the club's goal is to build a community that supports you to help you find your bliss, to identify what she calls "your through line" as you move forward.

Although Lesley didn't pursue a career in sustainability, because she pivoted into another opportunity she saw in front of her, she said she applies a lot of what she learned in school to her business—from technology to ways that she monetizes her business with membership fees and advertising support.

With CoveyClub running at full speed, and Lesley herself now in her early sixties, she also made another big decision in her life. After she and her husband raised their kids, they sold their house in a suburb of New York and moved to New Orleans, a city they had always loved. "It was just Jeff and me and two cats. If I had stayed in the house, it would remind me every day about being a mother, which is how I spent so much of my time doing that there. I couldn't move on without changing my environment," she explained. New Orleans gives them all that they want—from culture, music, and food to interesting people and ways to keep learning by accessing the universities there. Her community, or flock, can be connected to her from anywhere, but it is always helpful when you love where you live. Lesley has lots of plans to grow her covey well into the future.

Speaking of flocks, I'd like to tell you about two men who found a path in midlife toward an incredible commitment to service and community.

It took Father Mickey[7] more than forty years to realize that he had not acted on something he had been thinking about his whole life. At forty-four, he entered the priesthood, and five years later he was ordained as a Catholic priest. I was there to celebrate his ordination and his first mass. It had been a circuitous route, but nearly twenty-four years later, he continues to celebrate his decision, while he tends to his community of parishioners and those in need.

One of eight children in a big Irish Catholic family, he had gone to a Catholic high school and college and had always loved his Catholic identity and faith. He told me that even his grandmother used to say, "Keep an eye on Mickey: he is going to be a priest someday!"

Like many people, life took him on a different course. After college, he worked for IBM, but during that time, his younger brother was killed in a car crash. Father Mickey was left wondering if he himself was on the right course. In his early twenties, he quit his job and traveled to Calcutta, India, where he worked for two months with the Missionaries of Charity, the organization run by Mother Teresa. When he returned to the US, he headed home to his parents in Vermont, where he taught cross-country skiing, opened a stained-glass shop, and was hired by the Baroness Maria von Trapp (the real Maria from the musical *The Sound of Music*) to become a gardener at the Trapp Family Lodge in Stowe, Vermont.

Ultimately, Father Mickey moved to New York City and worked as a waiter and for a catering company, when a friend suggested he get into the modeling business, that his "guy next door" good looks might be a way for him to make some extra money. That idea led to thirteen years of "product modeling" for such brands as American Express, Citibank, and more. He did a stint living in Milan and crisscrossed the Atlantic for multiple modeling assignments. Yet the idea of priesthood was always in his mind, he told me, and finally one day he stepped onto the path that would take him there. Along the way, he obtained a master's degree in mental health counseling and became a CASAC (Credentialed Alcohol and Substance Abuse Counselor).

In 2005, Father Mickey heard a story about a young woman who was dying. Five years prior, she was engaged to be married, and on the night of the rehearsal dinner, the young couple was involved in a car accident. Her injuries were severe, and she was in desperate need of a kidney transplant. He said that upon hearing the story, he quietly went to the hospital and registered as "Mickey B." (without identifying himself as a priest), after learning that he might be a match. He donated his kidney, and fifteen years later, both donor and recipient are doing well. To me, that is the ultimate gift of service.

In his life's journey, Father Mickey has gone from parish priest to chaplain of a hospital to hospital ministry, and now he's at a nursing home and rehab facility. His life has been full and fulfilling. "I will never have nor do I want great wealth stored up in the bank. My wealth must come from within me," he said.

As he approaches seventy, Father Mickey thinks about what might be next for him. He dreams about starting a lavender farm when he retires someday, with his faith always being what guides him. "I am a late bloomer," he said. "The priesthood has been wonderful to me and I think I have been wonderful to the priesthood." Approaching twenty years as a priest, guiding a community of followers, Father Mickey is one of those lucky people who found his true calling when he was in his mid-forties. His courage and passion to realize what had been in his mind since boyhood made him the fullest of human beings.

Yet he has much left to do, citing one of his favorite poems, "Stopping by Woods on a Snowy Evening" by Robert Frost. Frost ends the poem with the line, "And miles to go before I sleep."[8]

My other story about reassessing your community and your relationship with it is about Fred Sievert,[9] a man I met when we served on a board together. A highly successful business executive, he had risen from a family of very modest means to become the president of New York Life, one of the largest life insurance companies in the United States. In his late fifties, he had begun to think about making a change by going to a divinity school, and he was coached by his minister as to how that path might progress.

At fifty-nine, he retired from his business career, saying that it was merely a prologue to what his life became as he moved forward. Fred enrolled at Yale Divinity School with strong support from his wife and five children. In doing so, he forged an amazing life that has given him huge personal growth and satisfaction.

Today, at seventy-two, Fred has spent a decade writing and speaking about his faith, what he calls his own form of ministry. He has written two books, *Grace Revealed: Finding God's Strength in Any Crisis* and *God Revealed: Revisit Your Past to Enrich Your Future.* He told me that his message has been delivered in more than seventy television and radio interviews, as well as thirty personal speaking engagements to large and small groups, including universities, book clubs, and prayer breakfast meetings. His service to his Christian community has resulted in ongoing communications with many of the people he has inspired and more than a million visits on StoriesofGodsGrace .com, his website of stories of others who have experienced an outpouring of God's grace.

"The peace of mind that has come from following my passions and impacting the lives of other people has literally left me far happier than I have been in many years," he told me, adding, "One of the truly amazing outcomes in this phase of my life has been a sense of youthfulness many years younger than my chronological age."

Do not conform to the pattern of this world, but be transformed by the renewing of your mind (Romans 12:2, New International Version).

Fred has ROARed into the second half of his life in a meaningful way. When he sent me a biblical passage, I thought it was apropos of his message: "Do not conform to the pattern of this world, but be transformed by the renewing of your mind" (Romans 12:2, New International Version).

ROAR TIP

Regardless of how you define service, you can only find true peace and satisfaction with yourself if you devote a part of your life to helping others. That simple idea has been taught, preached, written about, and passed on from generation to generation. It doesn't matter if you believe in a religion or not, you should always believe in somehow helping your fellow humans as one of the fundamentals of living.

The word *philanthropy* actually means "the love of mankind." Giving brings us personal happiness and joy, but many people don't know where to begin. First, you have to define your community. Are you among those who are passionate about addressing food insecurity, racial and social justice, helping underprivileged children, or wildlife preservation? What matters is what is important to you personally.

Next, you have to decide if you are going to give your time or your money or both. Start looking for nonprofit organizations that fulfill what excites you, and then become a part of their efforts. It could mean anything from volunteering at one of their fundraisers to joining their board of directors or making a financial donation. The amount of time or money is what you can afford, and they will be grateful for it.

According to Giving USA, individuals donated $292.09 billion to charities in 2018. The money went to religious institutions, education, human services, health organizations, environmental and animal organizations, and more.[10] As a people, Americans seem to have charity as part of their core DNA.

I've had the honor of serving on multiple nonprofit boards, including the Volunteers of America–Greater New York, the Starlight Children's Foundation, the International Center of Photography, and Pace University, to name a few. But my biggest sense of fulfillment came when some friends and I launched Circle of Generosity, a small foundation whose mission is to grant random acts of kindness to individuals and families in need. We help people who are facing an emergency, such as eviction or the loss of healthcare. We've helped people who were devastated by the floods in Houston, Baton Rouge, and New York. We have participated in global efforts at refugee camps and contributed to a fund to aid the widows of Sherpas killed in a devastating avalanche in 2014.

We like to say that we are the little engine that could, donating anywhere from $500 to $10,000, depending on the need. In 2020, we celebrated our tenth anniversary, acknowledging that during COVID-19, food insecurity was a particularly distressing issue, so we made a commitment to donate $50,000 in food vouchers and money to food pantries to help keep their shelves stocked.

The Circle of Generosity hosts an annual fundraiser, and it is our goal to give away all the money our supporters donate, while keeping our overhead to a tiny fraction of our costs. We have no paid employees, and our small board of eight people are volunteers and fundraisers. And we are on our way to giving away our first million dollars! It has been one of the most satisfying commitments of my life to be able to help strangers, anonymously, at a time when they are at their neediest, fulfilling my desire to embrace generosity as one of my core values.

My own interest in philanthropy led me to look for courses that I might take to learn more about the sector, which in turn led me to a master's program at Columbia University. I wasn't so sure that I wanted to become a student again in my sixties, particularly taking exams, writing papers, and sweating out a grade for a class. But I decided to apply, dredged up my college and graduate school transcripts, wrote an essay, and asked for references.

Once I was accepted, I told myself that I'd give it one semester to see if I liked it. One of the first courses was Ethics in Philanthropy, taught by Art Taylor, who also worked as the CEO of the Better Business Bureau Wise Giving Alliance. His class and lectures were so stimulating that it reignited my love of lifelong learning. And since I was planning to segue out of my publishing career, I realized that going back to school would provide the intellectual stimulation that would bridge me into a new world. (Actually, I was already in that world with my nonprofit boards and the Circle of Generosity, but this would put a punctuation mark on it.)

At sixty-seven, I became a proud graduate with a master's degree in nonprofit management, which included such courses as Innovations in Philanthropy and Planned Giving, as well as a deep dive into the world of nonprofits. For the rest of my life, I'll be engaged in the nonprofit sector as a president/founder, board member, advisor, and of course, donor. I may even go back to work full-time as the head of a nonprofit that excites me.

I'm passionate about the sector! I enjoyed learning about the incredible work of Muhammad Yunus, the Bangladeshi leader who was awarded the Nobel Peace Prize for founding the Grameen Bank and pioneering microfinancing and loans to those too poor to qualify for traditional ways to borrow money. I loved reading Dan Pallotta's book *Uncharitable: How Restraints on Nonprofits Undermine Their Potential.*

And I am following innovative social business models like Warby Parker, cofounded by a friend, Dave Gilboa. All of these examples highlight a sense of community that is inspiring.

The combination of business and social commitment is an exciting dimension of how we can all give back: by buying products from entities that include philanthropic contribution as part of their model. Younger adults, in particular, are motivated by buying from companies who are committed to giving back, and smart brands have now incorporated this into their mission

Social responsibility should be as relevant as the profit motive for corporations, as well as for the individuals who run them. It is part of the community commitment that we have to each other. In fact, the trade group Business Roundtable made a major announcement in 2019, signed by 181 CEOs of major corporations, that public companies not only have a responsibility to the profit motive, but also to having a broader corporate purpose for the well-being of their employees and the community at large.[11] This announcement was a watershed moment in the business world, because it recognized the importance of serving the wider community in addition to simply delivering a profit.

Aside from making the occasional donation to the charity of your choice, there are also lots of ways in which you can help your favorite cause. While you are alive, you can set aside money in your will for your favorite nonprofit or create a nonprofit beneficiary designation for your 401(k). Many kinds of instruments—such as charitable gift annuities and charitable remainder trusts—can provide you with life-time income and tax benefits while you are alive, as well as take care of one of your favorite charities.

Watching your money go to work in the community you are passionate about will bring you great joy and satisfaction throughout your life.

The key is to make sure that your selected charity is aware of your intent as a donor. Watching your money go to work in the community you are passionate about will bring you great joy and satisfaction throughout your life.

I write this final chapter on my birthday, which seems apropos, as birthdays are days when we should reflect on the year that has passed and dream about the year to come. What I know is that I'm eternally grateful for the life I have been able to live and for the commitments I have for the future: to always be curious as a lifelong learner, to always believe that all things are possible as an eternal optimist, and to be known as generous and loyal and honest and present with not only my family and friends, but with my community at large, which means anyone I meet on this road we call life.

> *To ROAR is to become the best you can be, as long as you walk this earth.*

To ROAR is to become the best you can be, as long as you walk this earth. To leave it a better place with your own contribution, or as some believe St. Augustine once wrote, "The key to immortality is first living a life worth remembering." Embrace what can be yours. Ask the question, *Why not me?* It's time to step forward, reimagineer—the second half of your life awaits you!

ROAR: Chapter Takeaways

- We are all one community, and it is our inherent responsibility to take care of each other as human beings. Every day can include some act of charity or goodwill to your fellow humans. Start practicing today! Ask yourself each night how you did on this front.
- Expressing ourselves is one of the key tenets of a democracy. We can disagree with each other, but we can listen to the other's point of view and try to find a common ground. Each of us can play our part to change divisiveness to harmony.
- The angels among us are those who start a mission to be of service to others, whether it is helping the disadvantaged or creating groups that help people create better lives. You can start a group or join a group. The key is to become a participant.

- Philanthropy is the love of mankind. It is more about the action than any amount you might donate. Become a volunteer, offer your skills to a nonprofit, start your own foundation. The key to a successful life is to give of yourself in some form to help others.
- Find your spiritual center, whether it is through a formal religion or your own form of being at one with the world and with the community around you. Be kind. Be generous. Be compassionate.

Conclusion

Now that you have embraced what it means to ROAR and have taken in how you too can start a new life, today is the day to begin. It doesn't matter how old you are, because you can begin at any age. In fact, it is something you should adopt as your manifesto for the rest of your life! While this book has told the stories of people from their forties to their eighties, so many of us are going to live well into our nineties, and some of us will hit one hundred!

In 2019, there were over 90,000 centenarians in the United States alone. That figure is expected to increase to 589,000 in the year 2060![1] And there will be many more people in their eighties and nineties who are going to redefine what it means to be "older." We will have to come up with better descriptors for them too, as they continue to find ways to reimagine what it is like to be a dynamic individual at that age. Actually, there are a lot of them among us already, including Johanna Quaas, the oldest active gymnast in the world at eighty-eight, the Japanese climber Yūichiro Miura, who climbed Mt. Everest at eighty, as well as my friend Carmen Dell'Orefice, who continues to model at age ninety!

Why limit your life with self-imposed ageist thinking that says, Oh, I can't do that, I'm too old?

So, if you think that making a major pivot at fifty is the end, it is actually the beginning of many other stages of reimagining that you will have to do in your life. You may have a twenty-year run in a new career until you are seventy, but then start another career that will last until you are ninety. You may have a second or even a third love in your life. Why not build a house at eighty or get a puppy at eighty-five? Why limit your life with self-imposed ageist thinking that says, *Oh, I can't do that, I'm too old*?

By embracing the ROAR manifesto and its lessons and tips, you open yourself up to all the possibilities that are before you until you leave this earth. Yes, there are many considerations. The first is are you maintaining a healthy lifestyle that affords you the ability to continue to grow? Keeping tabs on your health, a steady fitness regimen, good eating, and less stress and anxiety are several key building blocks that should top your list. That's your personal responsibility.

How much money will you need to live the life you want? As we all age, many of us are going to work at some income-generating job— some for the money but some for the stimulation. Companies and institutions are going to have to rethink how they hire, retrain, and support workers who are sixty-five plus. Those quaint and antiquated lists of "best jobs for people over fifty" are going to have to be torn up and replaced by more meaningful possibilities, knowing that someone age sixty could work for twenty years. Job opportunities should become more expansive in every field, and the entire culture has to stop promoting what someone over fifty is supposed to be like and what they are supposed to do. It means a complete reframing of how we think.

Reimagineers are going to decide that they do not want to be forced to leave their jobs or professions in their sixties. Some will opt out to become entrepreneurs, many will go back to school to learn something new, and many will do what I call the "reverse life." Instead of downsizing, they will upsize, not moving to Florida or Arizona but staying in their home states and cities. Assisted living will be redefined to avoid the ghettoization of our elders with old-fashioned notions that create depression and social isolation. Group housing and progressive communities can replace these institutions with upbeat attitudes and lifestyle approaches.

In 1970, Maggie Kuhn formed the Gray Panther movement because she was forced to retire at the age of sixty-five from her job at the Presbyterian Church. She lived to eighty-nine years old, fighting ageism and advocating for nursing home reform. She was an amazing woman who challenged the toxic thinking of what older people are supposed to be, taking on gerontologists, politicians, and the media.[2]

> *It's time for a louder voice in advocating for what should be new symbols and images of people, as they move deeper into the second and even the third act of their lives.*

While the movement is still in existence, it's time for a louder voice in advocating for what should be new symbols and images of people, as they move deeper into the second and even the third act of their lives, as well as legislation that is beneficial to older people. Age is a social justice issue that cuts across every race, ethnicity, and gender. Inclusiveness also means people over fifty, over sixty, and beyond.

Fortunately, there are battalions of individuals who see the opportunities they can tap into, regardless of their age. These are the role models for our future and the ones who will continue to show us that all things are possible.

ROAR is designed to help you become one of those very people. To move loudly into what will be the holistic approach to your life, one that brings you fulfillment, satisfaction, and joy. Become the example of what can be accomplished, not just for yourself but for your family, friends, and colleagues, as well as your children and grandchildren. The ROAR legacy may in fact become your life purpose, proving that we can all do anything—at any time.

> *The ROAR legacy may in fact become your life purpose, proving that we can all do anything—at any time.*

It's a way for you to be remembered that will impact generations of people to come, a contribution to what is the wonder of being human in its fullest possible way. Your noblest effort is to do this—until your last breath.

Acknowledgments

The idea of *ROAR* came together as I was preparing to wind down a forty-two-year publishing career and wanted to leave the extraordinary team at Hearst Magazines with some ideas to think about for their own professional and personal futures. To them, thank you for the years of collaboration, success, and high performance. You are truly the best in the industry!

As *ROAR* took on a life of its own, thank you to those who helped me on the journey to put together the message in this book. A special thanks to Michele and Richard Cohn, Linda Konner, Ruth Mills, Lindsay Easterbrooks-Brown, Emily Han, Norbert Beatty, and the team at Beyond Words and Simon & Schuster. A special thanks to Fran Crane, who for over thirty years has helped me keep it all together!

To those who read the manuscript as a work in progress, giving me invaluable input and ideas, thank you to Tom DeVincentis, Pamela Fiori, Jayne Jamison, Martha McCully, Kevin O'Malley, Erick Neher, and Chris Shirley. For their professional advice, thanks to Aimee Bell, Judith Bookbinder, Joanna Coles, Leigh Haber, Marta Hallett, Alison Levine, Rishad Tobaccowala, and Kate White.

A lot of people shared their stories for *ROAR*. To them and to those who have inspired me along the way, thanks to Helen Appleyard, Tom Arnott, Sade Baderinwa, Mickey Bancroft, Jeffrey Banks, Frank Bennack, Cathie Black, Susan Black, Randy Boyd, Walter Cain, David Carey, Duncan Chater, Debi Chirichella, Olivia Crane, Colleen Daly, Ginny Donohue, Michael Evans, Patricia Forehand, Jim Gath, Steve

Goodhue, Marty Gruber, Mike Hackney, Dawn Steele Halbert, Heather Idema, Marc Kaplowitz, Michael Kassan, Carol Kizis, Jack Kliger, Allison Kluger, Robin Koffler, Keith LaScalea, Maggie Lentz, Kate Lewis, Penny Lieberman, Keith Lieberthal, Jaqui Lividini, Don Loftus, Erik Logan, Jeanine Lombardi, Jeanne Marin, Julianna Margulies, Gil Maurer, Michelle Morris, Nadine McHugh, Cate Murden, McGarvey Black, Bob Oldakowski, Riccardo Orizio, Paul Pakusch, Anastasia Parsons, Richard Price, Lili Root, Valerie Salembier, Lesley Jane Seymour, Julia Shanahan, Elisabeth Schiraldi, Debra Shriver, Fred Sievert, Rob Smith, Fatima Latief Soeryonegoro, Deborah Soss, Steve Swartz, Dan Tyler, David Verklin, Kristine Welker, Stephanie Young, and Shelley Zallis.

ROAR could not have been written without the support of my family, who are always there cheering me on. A thanks to my father, Joseph, and in memory of my mother, Nancy, parents who have supported me throughout a lifetime of ideas and adventures. I'm forever grateful to Tom and Hannah, and to Kate, Clint, Shannon, Andy, Nicolas, Emerson, Matthew, Debbie, Sean, Luke, Paul, Chris, David, Joe, Peggy, Bob, Bobby, Janet, Kathleen, and in memory of my niece, Molly. I am always grateful to my group of friends, who all believe in *ROAR* and live their own lives to the fullest. Thanks to Adam, Andy, Cap, Chris, Chuck, Colleen, Emily, Haideh, Jay, Jonathan, Keith, Leslie, Marta, Marty, Pamela, Penny, Polly, Steve, Susie, and Todd.

Recommended Resources

Books

Throughout this book, I share some of my favorite authors and books that have inspired me and given me insight into living a life that ROARs. Here is a list of all those titles. Happy reading!

Deep Work: Rules for Focused Success in a Distracted World by Cal Newport
Die Broke: A Radical, Four-Part Financial Plan to Restore Your Confidence, Increase Your Net Worth, and Afford You the Lifestyle of Your Dreams by Stephen M. Pollan and Mark Levine
End of the Retirement Age: Embracing the Pursuit of Meaning, Purpose and Prosperity by David Kennedy
A Frenchwoman's Guide to Sex after Sixty by Marie de Hennezel
Getting Unstuck: How Dead Ends Become New Paths by Timothy Butler
Grace Revealed: Finding God's Strength in Any Crisis and *God Revealed: Revisit Your Past to Enrich Your Future* by Fred Sievert
Gray Dawn: How the Coming Age Wave Will Transform America—and the World by Peter G. Peterson
Hillbilly Elegy: A Memoir of a Family and Culture in Crisis by J. D. Vance
How to Retire with Enough Money: And How to Know What Enough Is by Teresa Ghilarducci
How to Win Friends and Influence People by Dale Carnegie
Hustle and Gig: Struggling and Surviving in the Sharing Economy by Alexandrea J. Ravenelle

Racing Age by Angela Jimenez

Retire Inspired: It's Not an Age, It's a Financial Number by Chris Hogan

Secrets of Longevity: Hundreds of Ways to Live to Be 100 by Dr. Maoshing Ni

60 Things to Do When you Turn 60: 60 Experts on the Subject of Turning 60 edited by Ronnie Sellers

Take the Leap: Change Your Career, Change Your Life by Sara Bliss

The Artist's Way: A Spiritual Path to Higher Creativity by Julia Cameron

The Grown Woman's Guide to Online Dating: Lessons Learned While Swiping Right, Snapping Selfies, and Analyzing Emojis by Margot Starbuck

The Happiness Curve: Why Life Gets Better after 50 by Jonathan Rauch

The Number: What Do You Need for the Rest of Your Life, and What Will It Cost? by Lee Eisenberg

The Power of Positive Thinking by Norman Vincent Peale

The Science of Positivity: Stop Negative Thought Patterns by Changing Your Brain Chemistry by Loretta Graziano Breuning, PhD

The Second Mountain: The Quest for a Moral Life by David Brooks

The Sleep Revolution: Transforming Your Life, One Night at a Time by Arianna Huffington

The Top Five Regrets of the Dying: A Life Transformed by the Dearly Departing by Bronnie Ware

Uncharitable: How Restraints on Nonprofits Undermine Their Potential by Dan Pallotta

What Color Is Your Parachute? For Retirement: Planning a Prosperous, Healthy, and Happy Future by John E. Nelson and Richard N. Bolles

Where You Go Is Not Where You'll Be: An Antidote to the College Admissions Mania by Frank Bruni

Younger Next Year: Live Strong, Fit, Sexy, and Smart—Until You're 80 and Beyond by Chris Crowley and Henry S. Lodge, MD

Websites and Organizations

There are plenty of online resources about living a fulfilling life as we age. To give you a sense, if you Google "second chapter of life," you'll find over one million results. During the writing and researching for this book, I came upon several interesting websites and resources that might offer you more pointers for your own self-exploration.

American Association of Retired Persons: aarp.org
The classic source for all things health, money, retirement, travel, and a whole lot more for people age fifty and over.

Harvard Advanced Leadership Initiative: advancedleadership
    .harvard.edu
A yearlong program for experienced leaders who want to apply their talents to solve significant social problems. Others include Exended Studies: Continuing and Professional Studies from the University of Nevada, Reno (extendedstudies.unr.edu), and the University of Minnesota Advanced Careers Initiative Fellows Program (umac.umn.edu).

Association of National Advertisers: ana.nct
A resource to look at the details of the SeeHer initiative.

Artgym: artgym.com
A company that focuses on people and leadership development through neuroscience and psychology of creative thinking.

Centers for Disease Control and Prevention: cdc.gov
A tool for various health calculators, including body mass index (BMI).

Tenzing Hillary Everest Marathon: everestmarathon.com
In case you want to try the ultimate adventure marathon.

Learn How to Become: learnhowtobecome.org
A site where you can find a complete guide to career changes over fifty and more.

Match: match.com
One of many types of dating sites for adults of all ages. Others include eharmony, SilverSingles, and Zoosk.

Vision boards: oprahmag.com/life/a29959841/how-to-make-a-vision
  -board/
A helpful article from *O, The Oprah Magazine* that explains how to create your own vision board, a tool to help you shape your future idea of yourself.

PUSH Mind & Body: pushmindandbody.com
A company designed to help people and businesses reach peak potential.

RichardStep: richardstep.com
A site with several personal tests and resources to enrich yourself and step up your career.

ScholarshipOwl: scholarshipowl.com
You can get a scholarship to study anything at any age. Use this as your resource to make your own dream come true.

Travelers' Century Club: travelerscenturyclub.org
If your desire is to visit one hundred countries, join this organization and share your adventures with other global travelers.

University Aviation Association: uaa.aero
If you want to fulfill that childhood dream of becoming a pilot, this is a helpful guide to over seven hundred aviation scholarships for people of any age.

Understand Myself: understandmyself.com
As a way to sharpen your own strengths and best attributes, take this test to see if you fit your own self-perception.

Wine & Spirit Education Trust: wsetglobal.com
The Wine & Spirit Education Trust is a globally recognized source for education and qualifications for wine professionals and enthusiasts.

World Health Organization: who.intextranet.who.int/agefriendlyworld
/who-network/

Check out the World Health Organization's global network for age-friendly cities and communities.

Wowzitude: wowzitude.com

A resource connecting communities through content and conversation for people fifty-five and over.

Notes

Introduction

1. Michael Clinton, "'ROAR into the Second Half of Your Life' Survey," June 2020, unpublished survey conducted by Hudson Valley Insights and fielded by Qualtrics's Research-Services. Hereafter this survey will be referred to in short form as the ROAR Into survey. Michael Clinton and his commissioned survey are not affiliated with ROAR, Inc., https://roarinc.com.

Chapter 1

1. Teacher, discussion with author, Spring 2020.
2. Polly, email correspondence with author, April 10, 2020.
3. Dawn Steele Halbert, interview with author, June 27, 2020.
4. Chris Latham, "Success Isn't Just for the Young," This Is Capitalism, accessed March 15, 2021, https://www.thisiscapitalism.com/success-isnt-just-for-the-young/.
5. Latham, "Success Isn't Just for the Young."
6. Latham, "Success Isn't Just for the Young."
7. David Nilssen, "Why Being 50 (or Older) Is Just Right for Entrepreneurship," *Entrepreneur*, June 2, 2014, https://www.entrepreneur.com/article/234401.
8. "Meet the Never-Retired: A Heavenly Coffee Grower," John Hancock (website), accessed March 15, 2021, https://www.johnhancock.com/ideas-insights/never-retired-coffee-grower.html.

9. Laura Bennett, "7 Incredible Women Over 50 Who Will Inspire You to Take That Risk," SeniorsMatter.com, accessed March 15, 2021, https://www.seniorsmatter.com/seven-incredible-women-over-50-who-will-inspire-you-to-take-that-risk/2491876.

10. Julianna Margulies, email correspondence with author, August 31, 2020.

11. Urban Zen, "Our Founder, Donna Karan," accessed March 15, 2021, http://urbanzen.org/.

12. Maggie Lentz, interview with author, June 6, 2020.

13. Jim Gath, interview with author, April 28, 2020.

14. Fatima Latief Soeryonegoro, email correspondence with author, October 19, 2020.

15. Helen Appleyard, email correspondence with author, October 22, 2020.

Chapter 2

1. "MRI-Simmons Fall 2020 Report," MRI-Simmons, accessed December 30, 2020, https://www.mrisimmons.com.

2. Robert J. Nash, "Why I Have Not Yet Retired," Inside Higher Ed, June 12, 2019, https://www.insidehighered.com/advice/2019/06/12/professor-who-has-taught-more-half-century-explains-why-he-hasnt-been-willing.

3. Gayle King, email correspondence with author, January 2021.

4. Jack Kliger, interview with author, June 29, 2020.

5. Susan Black, interview with author, October 17, 2020.

6. Ewing Marion Kauffman Foundation, "Who Is the Entrepreneur? Race and Ethnicity, Age, and Immigration Trends among New Entrepreneurs in the United States, 1996–2019," *Trends in Entrepreneurship* 9, July 6, 2020, http://www.kauffman.org/entrepreneurship/reports/race-ethnicity-age-immigration-trends-united-states-entrepreneurs-1996-2019/.

7. Sameeksha Desai (director of research, Ewing Marion Kauffman Foundation), discussion with author, November 24, 2020.

8. Nadine Karp McHugh, interview with author, Summer 2020.

9. Jeanine Lombardi, email correspondence with author, October 1, 2020.

10. David Verklin, discussion with author, August 2, 2020.

11. Rob Smith, interview with author, June 15, 2020.

12. Jonathan, interview with author, July 13, 2020.

13. Emily, discussion with author, August 10, 2020.

14. Julia, email correspondence with author, Summer 2020.

Chapter 3

1. David Carey, interview with author, June 28, 2020.
2. Órla Ryan, "The 'Oldest Street Photographer in Dublin' on Why It's Never Too Late to Change Careers," theJournal.ie, September 5, 2020, https://www.thejournal.ie/street-photography-dublin-5195499-Sep2020/.
3. Rebecca, discussion with author, Summer 2020.
4. *The Shawshank Redemption*, directed by Frank Darabont (Beverly Hills, CA: Castle Rock Entertainment, 1994), scene 293, accessed March 16, 2021, http://www.dailyscript.com/scripts/shawshank.html.
5. Cate Murden, interview with author, November 9, 2020.
6. Kristine Welker, interview with author, July 15, 2020.
7. Haaland "U.S. Secretary of the Interior—Secretary Deb Haaland," U.S. Department of the Interior, accessed May 19, 2021, https://www.doi.gov/secretary-deb-haaland; Clyde McGrady, "Haaland Recalls Struggles as Single Mom, Thanks-giving and Being Homeless," *Roll Call*, September 16, 2019, https://www.rollcall.com/2019/09/16/haaland-recalls-struggles-as-single-mom-thanksgiving-and-being-homeless/.
8. Matshona T. Dhliwayo, "To 15 Past, Present, & Future Quotes of all Time," Medium.com, August 8, 2017, https://medium.com/@matshonardhliwayo/top-15-past-present-future-quotes-of-all-time-by-matshona-dhliwayo-1f7236aa2ba8.

Chapter 4

1. Dr. Keith LaScalea, interview with author, August 12, 2020.
2. "Understanding Blood Pressure Readings," American Heart Association, accessed March 16, 2021, https://www.heart.org/en/health-topics/high-blood-pressure/understanding-blood-pressure-readings.
3. Fauja Singh marathon results, MarathonGuide.com, accessed March 16, 2021, http://www.marathonguide.com/results/search.cfm.
4. Martin Gruber, interview with author, August 17, 2020.
5. Board of Governors of the Federal Reserve System, "2019 Survey of Consumer Finances," in cooperation with the US Department of the Treasury, data collected by the NORC at the University of Chicago, accessed January 31, 2021, https://www.federalreserve.gov/econres/scfindex.htm.
6. Margaret and Bob Pardini, discussion with author, August 20, 2020.

7. Colette Thayer and Laura Skufca, "Do Images of Older Americans Reinforce Stereotypes?," AARP Research, AARP, September 2019, https://www.aarp.org/research/topics/life/info-2019/age-representation-in-online-media-images.html.

8. Dan Tyler, interview with author, June 14, 2020.

9. Sophia, interview with author, Summer 2020.

10. Joe Newman and Anita Sampson, "For Centenarian Survivor of 1918 Flu Pandemic, Coronavirus Is Just Another 'Problem,'" interview by Ailsa Chang, "Hunker Down Diaries," NPR, April 15, 2022, https://www.npr.org/transcripts/835131873.

11. Judith S. Lederman, "Pregnant at 53: Older Pregnancy Happened to Me," Parents.com, January 24, 2013, https://www.parents.com/getting-pregnant/age/pregnancy-after-35/pregnancy-age-pregnant-at-50/.

12. BJ Miller, "What Is Death? How the Pandemic Is Changing Our Understanding of Mortality," Opinion, *New York Times*, December 18, 2020, https://www.nytimes.com/2020/12/18/opinion/sunday/coronavirus-death.html.

Chapter 5

1. Erik Logan, interview with author, June 17, 2020.

2. Jeanne Marin (Jeanne Franck, MD), interview with author, August 19, 2020.

3. Northwoods Organic Produce, company Facebook page, https://www.facebook.com/Northwoods-Organic-Produce-523341721054870/.

4. Nancy Eike, "Urban Roots," *White Bear Lake Magazine*, April 2015, https://whitebearlakemag.com/urban-roots.

5. Bruce Horovitz, "Finding a New Job at Any Age: Traci Blackstock," *AARP The Magazine*, February/March 2016, https://www.aarp.org/work/job-hunting/info-2016/job-search-success-stories.html.

6. Riccardo Orizio, email correspondence with author, October 28, 2020.

7. Eugene Hughes, interview with author, October 30, 2020.

Chapter 6

1. Randy Boyd, interview with author, June 24, 2020.

2. Drive to 55 (history and stats), TN Achieves, accessed March 16, 2021, https://tnachieves.org/about-us/drive-to-55.

3. Office of the President: Randy Boyd, The University of Tennessee System, accessed March 16, 2021, https://president.tennessee.edu/biography/randy-boyd/.

4. The University of Tennessee Board of Trustees, https://trustees.tennessee.edu/wp-content/uploads/sites/3/2020/03/BOT-Meeting-Book-March-27-2020.pdf.

5. Colleen Daly, interview with author, July 6, 2020.

6. Michael Kassan, interview with author, August 20, 2020.

7. Paul Pakusch, interview with author, June 21, 2020.

8. Tom Arnott, discussion with author, August 11, 2020.

Chapter 7

1. Patricia Forehand, interview with author, June 13, 2020.

2. McGarvey Black, interview with author, June 30, 2020.

3. Michael Evans, interview with author, August 14, 2020.

4. Debra Shriver, interview with author, June 10, 2020.

5. Pamela, interview with author, May 26, 2020.

Chapter 8

1. Tom DeVIncentis, discussion with author, July 5, 2020.

2. Andrew Carter, discussion with author, August 1, 2020.

Chapter 9

1. Damjan Jugovic Spajic, "How Much Time Does the Average Person Spend on Their Phone?," Statistics, KommandoTech, February 11, 2020, https://kommandotech.com/statistics/how-much-time-does-the-average-person-spend-on-their-phone/.

2. Bronnie Ware, *The Top Five Regrets of the Dying* (New York: Hay House, Inc., 2019), 87.

3. Ware, *The Top Five Regrets of the Dying*, 127.

4. Don Loftus, interview with author, May 21, 2020.

5. Jeffrey Banks, email correspondence with author, July 8, 2020.

6. Mike Hackney, interview with author, June 26, 2020.

Chapter 10

1. Chuck, interview with author, August 15, 2020.
2. Anastasia Parsons, interview with author, July 10, 2020.
3. Michelle Morris, email correspondence with author, July 21, 2020.

Chapter 11

1. Marc Kaplowitz, interview with author, August 13, 2020.
2. Stephanie Young, interview with author, October 23, 2020.
3. "About Virginia Western: College Policies—1-32: Senior Citizens Higher Education Act of 1974," Virginia Western Community College, https://www.virginiawestern.edu/about/policies/I-32.php.
4. Walter Cain, interview with author, August 10, 2020.
5. Allison Kluger, interview with author, June 16, 2020.
6. Penny Ekstein-Lieberman, interview with author, September 12, 2020.
7. "50 Inspirational Quotes on Writing," Barnes & Nobel Press, January 4, 2021, https://press.barnesandnoble.com/bnpress-blog/inspirational-quotes-writing/.

Chapter 12

1. John Gramlich, "Young Americans Are Less Trusting of Other People—and Key Institutions—than Their Elders," Fact Tank News in the Numbers, Pew Research Center, August 6, 2019, https://www.pewresearch.org/fact-tank/2019/08/06/young-americans-are-less-trusting-of-other-people-and-key-institutions-than-their-elders/.
2. Gramlich, "Young Americans Are Less Trusting of Other People," Pew Research Center, https://www.pewresearch.org/fact-tank/2019/08/06/young-americans-are-less-trusting-of-other-people-and-key-institutions-than-their-elders/.
3. Edelman, "2020 Edelman Trust Barometer," accessed January 11, 2021, https://www.edelman.com/trust/2020-trust-barometer.
4. Ginny Donohue, interview with author, June 27, 2020.
5. Wikipedia, s.v. "Grandma Moses," last modified January 6, 2021, 11:31 AM, https://en.wikipedia.org/wiki/Grandma_Moses#cite_note-NYT_obit-1.
6. Lesley Jane Seymour, interview with author, August 17, 2020.

7. Father Mickey, interview with author, August 28, 2020.

8. Robert Frost, "Stopping by Woods on a Snowy Evening," Poetry Foundation, https://www.poetryfoundation.org/poems/42891/stopping-by-woods-on-a-snowy-evening.

9. Fred Sievert, email correspondence with author, August 29, 2020.

10. Giving USA, "Giving USA 2019: Americans Gave $427.71 Billion to Charity in 2018 amid Complex Year for Charitable Giving," accessed January 11, 2021, https://givingusa.org/giving-usa-2019-americans-gave-427-71-billion-to-charity-in-2018-amid-complex-year-for-charitable-giving/.

11. "Business Roundtable Redefines the Purpose of a Corporation to Promote 'An Economy That Serves All Americans,'" Business Roundtable, August 19, 2019, https://www.businessroundtable.org/business-roundtable-redefines-the-purpose-of-a-corporation-to-promote-an-economy-that-serves-all-americans.

Conclusion

1. Jiaquan Xu, MD, "Mortality among Centenarians in the Unites States, 2000–2014," National Center for Health Statistics, Centers for Disease Control and Prevention, January 2016, accessed January 11, 2021, https://www.cdc.gov/nchs/products/databriefs/db233.htm.

2. Emily Krichbaum, "Gray Panthers," *The Encyclopedia of Greater Philadelphia* (PhD dissertation, Rutgers University, 2020), https://philadelphiaencyclopedia.org/archive/gray-panthers/.

MICHAEL CLINTON is the former president and publishing director of Hearst Magazines and is currently special media advisor to the Hearst Corporation's CEO. He is also an author and photographer who believes that everyone should strive to live their fullest life possible—to optimize the second half of life. An avid traveler, Michael has experienced 124 countries and has run marathons on 7 continents. He is a private pilot and a part owner of a vineyard in Argentina, has started a nonprofit foundation, holds two master's degrees, and still has a long list of life goals and experiences he plans to tackle. He resides in New York and Santa Fe.